The Sporting News SELECTS
FOOTBALL'S 100 GREATEST PLAYERS

A Celebration of the 20th Century's Best

written by
Ron Smith

designed by
Bill Wilson

edited by
Carl Moritz

editor-in-chief
John Rawlings

FOREWORD BY JIM BROWN

CONTENTS

THE MAN BEHIND THE MUD IS FORMER PACKERS OFFENSIVE LINEMAN FORREST GREGG, NO. 28 ON TSN'S TOP 100 LIST.

KEY CONTRIBUTORS

Editorial Director
Steve Meyerhoff

Photographic Coordinator
Paul Nisely

Designer
Christen Webster

Prepress Project Coordinator
Jack Kruyne

OTHER CONTRIBUTORS

Selection Committee
Paul Attner, Dennis Dillon, Steve Gietschier, Joe Hoppel, Carl Moritz, Mike Nahrstedt,
Dan Pompei, John Rawlings, Dave Sloan, Ron Smith, Sean Stewart, Kyle Veltrop

Copy Editors
Dennis Dillon, Dave Sloan, Sean Stewart

Special Writer
Bill Ladson

Timeline
Craig Carter

Timeline Graphic
Mike Nyerges

Prepress Specialists
David Brickey, Vern Kasal, Steve Romer, Ian Wilkinson

ISBN: 0-89204-624-4

10 9 8 7 6 5 4 3 2 1

INTRODUCTION

hen 12 editors of *The Sporting News* began selecting the best 100 pro football players of the century, nobody could have envisioned the range of opinion, the gnashing of teeth and the spirited arguments that would take place over a sometimes-painful six-week process. The responsibility was not taken lightly; the panelists worked hard to pare an original list of thousands to a select few and came away from the exercise with a healthier respect for the history of a sport that doesn't always take the time to look back.

It seems only fitting that TSN should be the publication to punctuate the centennial with a ranking of 100 players, a list that coincides with the beginning of the National Football League in 1920. TSN, the only pre-1900 sports weekly still in existence, has chronicled the professional game from its early days, watching, analyzing, criticizing and describing events for millions of readers.

The selection committee eventually established a list of about 300 names—every Hall of Fame player and numerous players who competed at a near-Hall of Fame level—to begin the ranking process. The first task was to cull that list to the 100 names that would appear in the book.

Every editor was then asked to pick a Top 10, without rankings. After those votes were tabulated and the Top 10 was locked in place, each voter was asked to rank those players and select the next 15 to fill out a Top 25. This selection process was continued for 26-50, 51-75 and 76-100, always locking the players into a group before rankings were determined. The group breakdowns prevented one voter with a low opinion of an otherwise well-regarded player from skewing that player's place in the rankings.

The voters were armed with clip files, statistical books, historical knowledge, personal observations and, of course, strong opinions that helped in their selections. The final rankings, obviously subjective and open to debate, represent the collective feelings of a TSN staff that has logged many hours tracking the course of football history.

The profiles that appear in the book attempt to provide a quick glimpse into the player's personality and playing style. The lists and charts that accompany each profile provide a competitive perspective you can't get from other sources.

A special thanks to all the former players, coaches and executives who responded so enthusiastically to our invitation to contribute the Top 10 lists that appear throughout the book.

FOREWORD

BY JIM BROWN

I don't really like awards, but being named the NFL's greatest player by *The Sporting News* makes me feel proud. When I think of Jim Brown the football player, I think about his attitude. You love the game and you know the coaches don't want you to miss a game.

One time I broke my toe, and the coaches asked, "Do you want to have the doctor look at it?" I said, "There's no point in the doctor looking at the toe because you guys want me to play anyway. If he says I can't play, you are going to be unhappy." I'm not telling you this for bravado; it's the nature of the game. You always could sit out if you want to have an excuse. My thing was, I played for me—my dignity, pride and goals. I didn't need to read the newspapers. I didn't need the accolades. I knew when I did the job and when I didn't.

I didn't pattern my game after a running back. When I was growing up, I liked Joe DiMaggio and Jackie Robinson. I liked the style of DiMaggio—the grace, the attitude and the rhythm. And I liked the overall attitude of Robinson, when he broke the color line in baseball—keeping his mouth closed, performing under adverse conditions. Later on, he was one of the most outspoken people in sports.

When you analyze my NFL career, you can't just look at the yardage and touchdowns. You have to look at the whole package. I never missed a game, I went to practice every day. The Cleveland Browns were contenders, I played for the championship three times in nine years and I never stayed over my time limit. I was 29 years old when I retired.

I don't think about the records I could have held if I continued to play football. Records are irrelevant. I know the product has to be hyped in order to create excitement for people. But certain things that count to championship teams do not result in records. Sometimes 1 yard at the right time makes the difference between winning and losing. But they don't have any records for 1-yard carries.

In order to be a successful running back, you must have quickness and intelligence. In other words, you must have the whole package. But even if you have the whole package, you must be in the right system. A coach must give you the ball, design plays for you and make adjustments from week-to-week. When Blanton Collier became my coach in 1963, he gave me the sweeps that I wanted. And every time a great running back runs a sweep, there's a good chance of breaking away. When you get a great back who hits that corner and finds the alley, the opposition is going to be in trouble.

There was another play I loved called "option blocking," where our offensive line would take the defensive player anywhere it wanted and I would pick my hole. When Blanton put in option blocking, I averaged about 6.5 yards per carry. It was the greatest thing that ever happened to me.

I wouldn't have been a success without the Browns' offensive line. I had Dick Schafrath and Gene Hickerson, who should be in the Hall of Fame. My line also blocked for Leroy Kelly. So we have two Hall of Fame running backs and don't have a member of the offensive line enshrined in Canton, Ohio. We had the best downfield blockers in the history of professional football—Schafrath, Hickerson, John Wooten, Monte Clark. These guys were dedicated individuals who would take direction and execute to the best of their abilities. I credit them for the overall success of the team and my career.

I have admiration for so many running backs. I always evaluate them on their particular ability, never measure them against anybody else. When you talk about today's running backs, Barry Sanders is the most talented in the league. Terrell Davis is not as gifted as Barry, but in the context of their teams, Terrell is more gifted than Barry. Terrell and Emmitt Smith have been able to lift their teams to the Super Bowl level.

Finally, I'm really proud of the people who selected me as the NFL's greatest player. They really had to do a lot of research and deal with their souls. So many times in my life, people haven't done their homework and have made assumptions. Somebody had to look at my career in the true form and make a decision. I feel very good about that.

Jim Brown

H e came, he saw, he conquered. And then, like a thief in the night, he disappeared from professional football with every rushing record known to man. Many have been re-established, but the legend

of Jim Brown remains as powerful as the body-scattering runs that lifted him to prominence as the Cleveland Browns' ultimate offensive weapon from 1957 to '65. He was, simply, the greatest pure runner in the history of the NFL.

Brown was a physical masterpiece, a gift from the football gods. His 18-inch neck, wide shoulders and 45-inch chest tapered down to a 32-inch waist and massive thighs that carried him around the field with the grace and power of a jaguar. Brown ran with head high, nostrils flaring, legs pumping and powerful arms swatting away tacklers like flies. He was an amazing combination of power and speed who could juke past slower defenders or run over linebackers and defensive backs.

A multisport star at Syracuse, he stormed through the NFL as a 1957 rookie, running for 942 yards and posting the first of eight rushing championships he would claim over a nine-year career. His yearly rushing totals would become the standard for future runners to aspire: 1,527, 1,329, 1,257, 1,408, 1,863, 1,446 and 1,544. The beauty of Brown was that everybody knew he was going to get the ball, and the opposing team still couldn't stop him.

The nine-time Pro Bowl choice was equally intimidating off the field, where his menacing glares, in-your-face attitude and outspoken views often were interpreted as resentful

and rebellious. He played the game without emotion, the same way he delivered the shocking 1965 news that he would retire, at age 29, while filming a movie in London. He left at the top of his game, the proud owner of one championship ring (1964) and 20 NFL records that included rushing yards (12,312), yards per carry (5.2) and rushing touchdowns (106).

BEST PLAYERS I'VE SEEN

SELECTED BY DEACON JONES

1. Jim Brown
2. Jim Parker
3. Sammy Baugh
4. Sid Luckman
5. Johnny Unitas
6. Otto Graham
7. Bobby Layne
8. O.J. Simpson
9. Chuck Bednarik
10. Marion Motley

1

JIM BROWN

"HE TOLD ME, 'MAKE SURE WHEN
ANYONE TACKLES YOU HE REMEMBERS
HOW MUCH IT HURTS.' HE LIVED BY
THAT PHILOSOPHY AND I ALWAYS
FOLLOWED THAT ADVICE."

JOHN MACKEY, 1999

"IF YOU PUT (THE
BALL) OUT THERE
ANYWHERE NEAR HIM,
HE'LL ADJUST
AT FULL SPEED
AND GET IT.
WITH HIM, YOU CAN
CONCENTRATE ON
THE REST OF THE
PLAY; THE THROW IS
THE EASIEST PART."

FORMER 49ERS
QUARTERBACK JEFF
KEMP, 1986
THE SPORTING NEWS

2

JERRY RICE

I t's hard not to notice Jerry Rice. He's an eye-catching combination of size, speed and agility—the long-armed No. 80 who reaches over the top of defenders to make a catch or blows past them with graceful explosiveness.

He's a marked man, the player every defensive game plan has been designed to stop for 14 NFL seasons. But no secondary has been able to accomplish that feat against "the best receiver in football history."

Rice doesn't just beat defensive backs, he destroys them. He's fearless over the middle, sure-handed in a crowd and fluid in patterns with an extra gear that gives him separation from swift cornerbacks. Rice is not a sprinter, but he has what former San Francisco teammate Ronnie Lott calls "game speed," the ability to explode into the open when it matters most—on Sundays. And he has big, soft hands that pluck passes effortlessly.

A workaholic who is obsessive about running routes with absolute precision, Rice also is known for his grueling offseason workout routine. It's no coincidence that Rice's chiseled 196-pound body has been durable, whether he's operating as equal parts possession receiver, gamebreaker and blocker. Or that his quiet intelligence has been a perfect fit for the sophisticated 49ers offense and quarterbacks Joe Montana and Steve Young. It all revolves around a sterling work ethic.

The numbers are hard to fathom. As he enters the 1999 season, Rice owns virtually every major receiving record, regular or postseason. His 17,612 receiving

yards are 3,608 ahead of his nearest challenger; his 1,139 catches are 199 ahead; he has 164 receiving touchdowns, 12 1,000-yard seasons, season highs of 1,848 yards and 122 catches. "He is not a normal

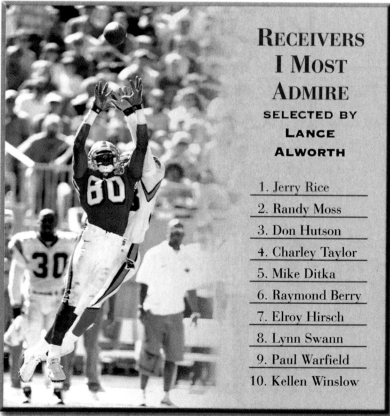

RECEIVERS I MOST ADMIRE
SELECTED BY LANCE ALWORTH

1. Jerry Rice
2. Randy Moss
3. Don Hutson
4. Charley Taylor
5. Mike Ditka
6. Raymond Berry
7. Elroy Hirsch
8. Lynn Swann
9. Paul Warfield
10. Kellen Winslow

human being," former teammate Randy Cross once said. Rice, a 12-time Pro Bowl selection and Super Bowl MVP, also has been a member of three 49ers championship teams.

3
JOE MONTANA

His gunslinger name fit the calm, calculating manner in which he shot down opposing defenses. It was part of the Joe Montana charisma, a mystique that permeated the NFL for 15 successful seasons. He was Joe Cool, the man who revived a franchise, carved out a Super Bowl legacy and built a reputation as the greatest pressure quarterback of all time.

Montana was a football surgeon, an artist who could carve up a defense with patience and relentless precision. His arm strength and speed were only slightly above average, but his quick feet and quicker mind were perfect matches for San Francisco and coach Bill Walsh's complicated short-passing offense. He seemed to have a sixth sense that allowed him to evade rushers and could throw on the run with uncanny, mistake-free accuracy.

Montana, who piled up big yardage, high completion percentages and victories while throwing to Jerry Rice and a host of other talented receivers in the 1980s, might have combined all aspects of quarterback play better than anyone in history. He was a great passer (40,551 yards in his career, 5,772 in postseason play), a dangerous scrambler (1,676 yards, 20 touchdowns), a masterful play-caller and an unquestioned leader. While assembling a 92.3 career passer rating (second to Steve Young on the NFL list), Montana took the postseason-

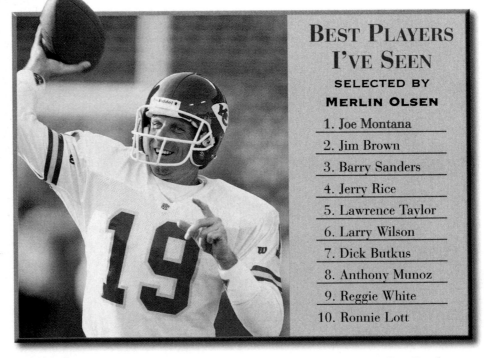

starved 49ers to four Super Bowls, won them all and claimed a record three MVPs.

The image of Montana, executing a near-perfect drive in the final moments of a big game, will forever be etched in the fabric of NFL history. He led 31 fourth-quarter comeback victories, including playoffs, and his late-game heroics lifted teammates to higher

BEST PLAYERS I'VE SEEN
SELECTED BY
MERLIN OLSEN

1. Joe Montana
2. Jim Brown
3. Barry Sanders
4. Jerry Rice
5. Lawrence Taylor
6. Larry Wilson
7. Dick Butkus
8. Anthony Munoz
9. Reggie White
10. Ronnie Lott

performance levels. When the eight-time Pro Bowl selection left San Francisco after an almost two-year layoff with elbow problems, he came back and led Kansas City to the AFC championship game before retiring after the 1994 season.

"I JUST HOPE NOW THEY'LL STOP SAYING, 'HE'S RIGHT UP THERE WITH THE BEST.' HE'S THE GREATEST BIG-GAME PLAYER I'VE SEEN, PERIOD."

FORMER 49ERS CENTER RANDY CROSS,
AFTER SUPER BOWL XXIII, 1989

"WHEN GOD CREATED A RUNNING BACK, HE CREATED WALTER PAYTON. WHEN HE CREATED AN OUTSIDE LINEBACKER, HE CREATED LAWRENCE TAYLOR."

LONGTIME NFL ASSISTANT COACH
JOHNNY ROLAND

4

LAWRENCE TAYLOR

Hall of Famers shook their heads in disbelief, opponents eyed him with nervous anticipation and fans marveled at the way he threw big, tough players around like rag dolls. When Lawrence Taylor stepped onto the field, everybody noticed. The riveting eyes, imposing glare and intimidating, perfectly sculpted body were merely appetizers for the savage rage he would unleash on every play.

Taylor's reputation was such that he could disrupt a game plan without moving one of the well-defined muscles on his 6-3, 237-pound frame. New York Giants opponents would look for him out of the corners of their eyes, listen for him and sense his presence. Linemen forgot counts, quarterbacks dropped snaps and blockers jumped offside. When LT did go into action, he could dominate capable linemen, chase down ballcarriers on both sides of the field and fight through triple-team blocks to record one of his patented quarterback takedowns.

Taylor jumped into the NFL spotlight quickly, earning NFL defensive player of the year honors as a rookie in

1981. By his second season, he already had become the standard by which future linebackers would be judged. He made pass rushing a function of the position and literally changed the way defense was played,

prompting former Raiders coach John Madden to call him "the most dominant defensive player I've ever seen."

His search-and-destroy abilities were fueled by an anger that might someday be matched but never surpassed. He produced sacks in double digits for seven consecutive seasons (1984-1990), including 20½ in 1986, when the Giants advanced to their first Super Bowl title and Taylor was named NFL Player of the Year by The Sporting News. He is the only defensive player to win the award.

With Taylor as a driving force, the Giants also won the Super Bowl after the 1990 season and reached the playoffs seven times in his 13 seasons. He finished his career in 1993 with 10 Pro Bowl citations and 132½ sacks.

BEST PLAYERS I'VE SEEN
SELECTED BY RONNIE LOTT

1. Jim Brown	6. Barry Sanders
2. Joe Montana	7. Reggie White
3. Jerry Rice	8. John Elway
4. Walter Payton	9. Joe Greene
5. Lawrence Taylor	10. Dick Butkus

5 JOHNNY UNITAS

The distinctive stoop shoulders were sandwiched by crew-cut hair and black, high-top shoes. You couldn't help but pick Johnny Unitas out of a football crowd. And you couldn't help but admire his extraordinary ability to pick apart defenses with commanding, unwavering confidence. He never backed down from anybody over 18 NFL seasons, building an unsurpassed reputation for toughness while gaining status as one of the most fabled stars in league history.

Johnny U. was a master craftsman, an unlikely looking athlete who overcame physical limitations with impressive intangibles. He wasn't fast, but he knew when and how to run. His arm was not as strong as some, but he threw with remarkable touch and timing. Most of all, Unitas had courage, coolness under fire and the ability to lead, a quality Baltimore teammate John Mackey acknowledged when he said, "It's like being in the huddle with God."

The no-nonsense Unitas was a pocket passer who was peerless when it came to standing in against the rush and delivering the ball at the last instant before contact. He also was a play-calling genius who could mentally dissect a defense, make the perfect audible and get the ball to the right player. He was in complete command when a game was on the line and was masterful at driving his team against the clock, an ability that vaulted him into prominence when he led the Colts to their classic overtime victory over the New York Giants in the 1958 title game.

Unitas was the most decorated passer in history when he retired in 1973 after one season in San Diego. He left with then-record totals of 2,830 completions, 40,239 yards and 290 touchdowns, but he'll always be remembered for the 47 straight games in which he threw at least one TD pass— a still-standing record. Johnny U., a 10-time Pro Bowl choice, played on four NFL championship teams and one Super Bowl loser.

TOUGHEST QBs TO DEFEND
SELECTED BY SAM HUFF

1. Johnny Unitas	6. Fran Tarkenton
2. Sonny Jurgensen	7. Bart Starr
3. Y.A. Tittle	8. Dan Marino
4. Bobby Layne	9. Billy Kilmer
5. Norm Van Brocklin	10. Joe Namath

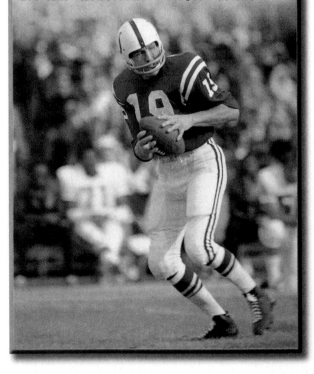

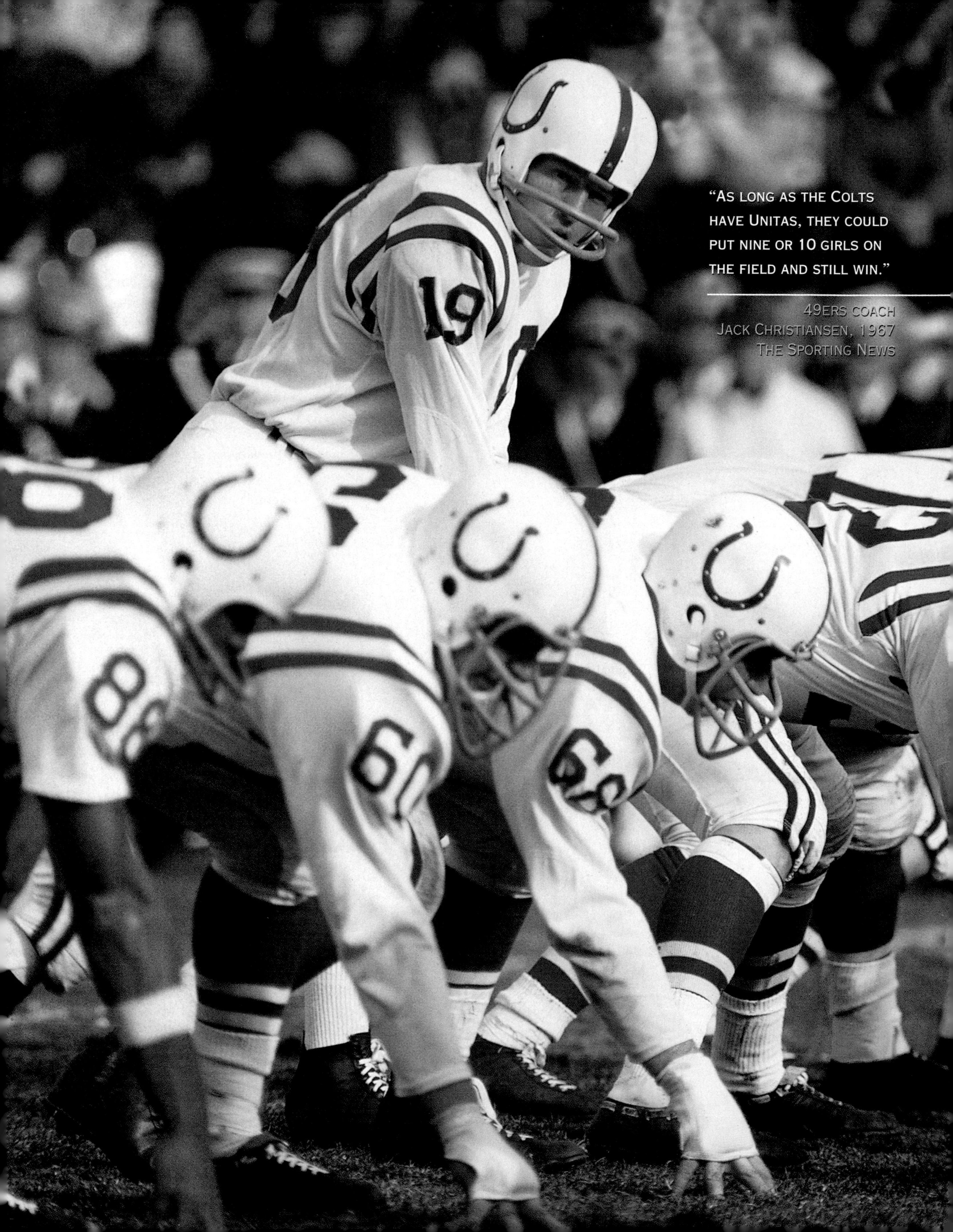

"As long as the Colts have Unitas, they could put nine or 10 girls on the field and still win."

49ers coach
Jack Christiansen, 1967
The Sporting News

6 DON HUTSON

He was a gift from the future, a premonition in helmet and cleats. To say Don Hutson was ahead of his time is well beyond understatement. Hutson was professional football's first great

receiver, a pass-catching pioneer who helped map the course the game would follow through the second half of the 20th century.

Hutson, the star of Alabama's 1935 Rose Bowl winner, was the worst nightmare for NFL coaches accustomed to defensing the conservative single-wing offenses of the era. He was tall (6-1), elusive and fast—that rare athlete who could find an extra gear and explode past helpless defensive backs. Hutson also could outleap most defenders and his big hands and long reach turned poorly thrown passes into highlight-film touchdowns. Football fans marveled at the sight of Hutson pulling in long passes and loping gracefully into the end zone.

Hutson was the centerpiece for Green Bay coach Curly Lambeau's innovative quick-strike offense from 1935 to '45. Over his 11-year career, he led

RECEIVERS I MOST ADMIRE
SELECTED BY PAUL WARFIELD

1. Don Hutson	6. Lance Alworth
2. Jerry Rice	7. Raymond Berry
3. Bobby Mitchell	8. Steve Largent
4. Charley Taylor	9. Kellen Winslow
5. John Mackey	10. Charlie Joiner

the league in receptions eight times and touchdown catches on nine occasions. His season receiving yardage totals consistently topped opposing team totals and most of that yardage was compiled while battling double- and triple-team coverage—unheard of strategy at the time. When he recorded the NFL's first 1,000-yard season (1,211) in 1942, 17 of his record 74 catches went for touchdowns.

When Hutson retired, his 488 career catches dwarfed the 298 total of his nearest competitor. His 99 TD receptions stood as a record for many years, as did his 16.4-yard average. His offensive greatness (he once scored 29 points in a quarter) was complemented by his prowess as a defensive back (30 interceptions) and kicker (193 points). A member of three Green Bay championship teams, he became a charter member of the Hall of Fame in 1963.

"I'D ALWAYS DREAMED OF AN END WHO
COULD DO THE THINGS HUTSON DID. AND
OUT AT PRACTICE (FOR THE ROSE BOWL)
AT PASADENA THAT DAY, THERE HE WAS."

CURLY LAMBEAU, ON HIS
FIRST SIGHTING OF DON HUTSON

7

OTTO GRAHAM

He was the perfect quarterback for the near-perfect franchise. What Otto Graham lacked in arm and physical strength, he more than made up for with uncanny throwing accuracy, poise and leadership.

He was a winning machine— the generator that powered the newborn Cleveland Browns through their incredible first decade as a professional football team.

Automatic Otto was just that from 1946 through 1949 when he led the Browns to a 47-4-3 record

SMARTEST QUARTERBACKS

SELECTED BY GEORGE BLANDA

1. Otto Graham
2. Bart Starr
3. Joe Montana
4. Terry Bradshaw
5. Johnny Unitas
6. Norm Van Brocklin
7. Bobby Layne
8. John Elway
9. Roger Staubach
10. Bob Waterfield

and four straight championships in the All-America Football Conference, and from 1950 to '55 when his Browns captured three NFL titles and lost three other times in the title game. Ten straight championship-game appearances and a 105-17-4 10-year record are legacies unmatched by any other quarterback.

Graham, a former basketball and football star at Northwestern and a one-year professional in the old National Basketball League, was a clever ballhandler who was handpicked by franchise architect Paul Brown as the centerpiece for his innovative T-formation offense. The 6-1, 195-pound Graham became a master on-field tactician who always seemed to make the right decision. Game after game, he would scramble for the unexpected yards, drop soft, easy-to-catch passes over the shoulders of receivers and make the big play at a crucial moment.

Everything about Graham was precision and confidence—and never was his poise more evident than when the Browns, undisputed champions of the outlaw AAFC, made the difficult 1950 move to the stronger NFL. Graham passed the Browns to a humbling debut victory over defending-champion Philadelphia, a first-year championship and instant respect. Blessed with an outstanding corps of running backs and receivers, he went on to post career totals of 23,584 passing yards (AAFC and NFL combined) and 174 touchdown passes in an era still dominated by power running attacks.

"THE TEST OF A QUARTERBACK IS WHERE HIS TEAM FINISHES. BY THAT STANDARD, OTTO WAS THE BEST OF THEM ALL."

PAUL BROWN

"IT'S HIS LEGS. HE'S GOT THE STRONGEST LEGS
I'VE EVER SEEN. THEY ARE LIKE SPRINGS. ...
IF HE HAD PLAYED ON GOOD TEAMS, OH MY GOSH,
I CAN'T IMAGINE WHAT HE WOULD HAVE DONE."

BOBBY BEATHARD, 1984
THE SPORTING NEWS

8 WALTER PAYTON

Sweetness was an illusion nurtured by Chicago Bears fans who watched Walter Payton perform for 13 NFL seasons. Blurred by the 16,726 yards he piled up as the most prolific runner in football history were the

thousands of bruises, headaches and battered egos he left on his record-setting trail of tears. There was nothing sweet about Payton's running style, which reflected hard work, hustle, enthusiasm and total effort.

Every Payton run started with the trademark first-step burst that carried him into the hole, where he could accelerate to daylight or explode into a tackler with aggressive, punishing force. Every Payton run ended with the 5-10, 200-pounder grinding, scrapping, fighting, battling for one more yard. No one in history ran harder, play after play, and nobody did more with modest speed than the blue-collar star former Bears coach Mike Ditka called "the most complete football player I ever saw."

Superbly conditioned, Payton also was an outstanding receiver and a threat to break open a game with the halfback pass, which he threw eight times for touchdowns. Need a block? Payton could deliver with the fierce drive of a fullback, a role he relished even more than his ball-carrying exploits. His powerful legs and sledgehammer arms were feared weapons, as was the delight he took in clearing a hole or protecting his quarterback.

A playful, fidgety clubhouse prankster, Payton became a yardage machine when he pulled on his No. 34 jersey. Among his 77 100-yard performances was a record 275-yard effort in 1977 against the Vikings and his 21,264 combined rushing/receiving yards

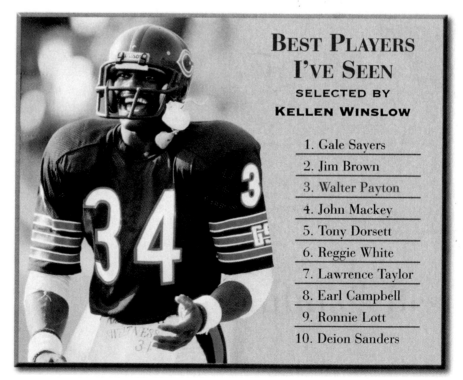

BEST PLAYERS I'VE SEEN
SELECTED BY
KELLEN WINSLOW

1. Gale Sayers
2. Jim Brown
3. Walter Payton
4. John Mackey
5. Tony Dorsett
6. Reggie White
7. Lawrence Taylor
8. Earl Campbell
9. Ronnie Lott
10. Deion Sanders

accounted for 125 touchdowns, 110 on the ground. Payton, a nine-time Pro Bowl choice who missed only one game in a career that ended in 1987, earned his only championship ring when the 1985 Bears defeated New England in Super Bowl XX.

"If I had a choice, I'd sooner go one-on-one with a grizzly bear. I pray that I can get up every time Butkus hits me."

FORMER NFL RUNNING BACK
MACARTHUR LANE

9

DICK BUTKUS

He was a grunting, snarling, snorting defensive machine, dedicated to the creation of football mayhem and the destruction of offensive game plans. Dick Butkus' road to the Hall of Fame was paved with blood, sweat, pain—and the intense anger that coursed through the veins of the most celebrated middle linebackers.

The 6-3, 245-pound Butkus served as the Chicago Bears' defensive leader and enforcer from 1965 to '73, when the almost-constant physical pounding finally took its toll on a body that had been pushed to full throttle on every play. He was both loved and hated for the mean, take-no-prisoners style he brought to the field, but his success was fueled by a consuming drive to be the best and a relentless dedication to his profession.

The burly, blue-collar Butkus combined surprising speed with a fearsome strength that he used to fight off powerful blockers. A ballcarrier who fell into the grasp of his long, thick arms could expect to be squeezed into helpless submission. Other runners and offensive linemen were constantly amazed by the ferocity of his hits. Butkus could run down ballcarriers from sideline-to-sideline, cover receivers out of the backfield and make the right calls for coach George Halas' complicated defense.

Butkus' misfortune was that he played for weak Chicago teams that never challenged for NFL superiority. But he played in eight Pro Bowls and the acclaim—and notoriety—he gained beyond his hometown of Chicago reached legendary status. Butkus' incredible instinct for the ball can be documented by the 25 opponent fumbles he recovered and the 22 interceptions he recorded in 119

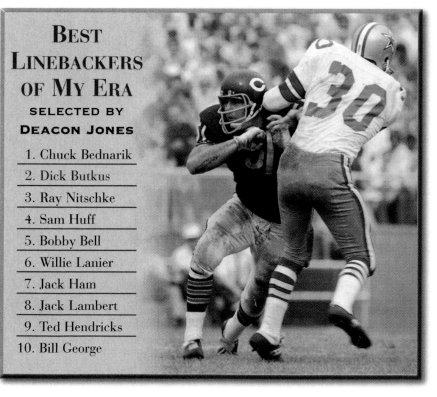

BEST LINEBACKERS OF MY ERA
SELECTED BY **DEACON JONES**

1. Chuck Bednarik
2. Dick Butkus
3. Ray Nitschke
4. Sam Huff
5. Bobby Bell
6. Willie Lanier
7. Jack Ham
8. Jack Lambert
9. Ted Hendricks
10. Bill George

professional games. He also is known as one of best ball-stripping tacklers in league history, having the uncanny ability to make a tackle with one arm and knock the ball free with the other.

"I'VE SAID THIS BEFORE AND I'LL SAY IT AGAIN. IN MY LIFETIME, THERE HASN'T BEEN A PLAYER AS GOOD AS LILLY. AND I DON'T EXPECT EVER TO SEE ANOTHER ONE. HE IS THAT ONCE-IN-A-LIFETIME PLAYER."

TOM LANDRY

10

BOB LILLY

H e is known affectionately as Mr. Cowboy—the first draft pick in Dallas franchise history, the team's first All-Pro, first Pro Bowl selection, first Ring of Honor member and first Hall of Famer.

But Bob Lilly also is known in many football circles as the greatest defensive tackle ever to put on a uniform, the centerpiece for the late-1960s Doomsday defenses that helped an expansion team reach championship heights.

Lilly was a 6-5, 260-pound time bomb that exploded into furious action every time the ball was snapped. Nobody his size could match the combination of incredible strength and quickness that allowed him to fight through blocks, chase down ballcarriers from sideline-to-sideline and pressure quarterbacks into errant throws. Double- and triple-team blocking schemes failed to neutralize Lilly's furious rush and many a competent blocker was brushed aside like a giant gnat.

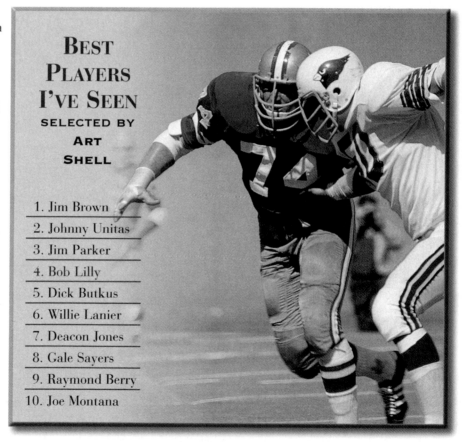

BEST PLAYERS I'VE SEEN

SELECTED BY
ART SHELL

1. Jim Brown
2. Johnny Unitas
3. Jim Parker
4. Bob Lilly
5. Dick Butkus
6. Willie Lanier
7. Deacon Jones
8. Gale Sayers
9. Raymond Berry
10. Joe Montana

An All-American at Texas Christian University, Lilly was the foundation upon which an expansion powerhouse was built. He arrived in 1961 with his sleepy, country-boy looks and began a 14-season run in which he never missed a regular-season game while earning 11 Pro Bowl selections and a remarkable eight All-NFL citations.

Lilly was a student of the game, a player who constantly studied film and worked to improve his technique. What he might have lacked in intensity he more than made up for with hard work and a desire to be the best. As the team's talent level rose quickly in the mid-1960s, so did his championship hopes—aspirations that were fulfilled with six NFL/NFC title game appearances, two Super Bowl appearances and a championship after the 1971 season.

11

SAMMY BAUGH

"I LIKE TO JUST SIT AND WATCH HIM. EVERY TIME HE THROWS, I LEARN SOMETHING. BUT NOBODY IS EVER GOING TO EQUAL HIM. NOT ANYBODY."

SID LUCKMAN, 1950

He blew through 1937 Washington like a twister off the West Texas plains. The tall, skinny, pin-legged kid with the shy drawl and powerful right arm ravaged conservative opponents while putting his new city on the NFL map and the professional game on a fast track toward innovation.

Sammy Baugh, a 6-2, 182-pound All-American from Texas Christian University, was everything he was cracked up to be—in performance, if not looks.

Slingin' Sammy, a poised and confident rookie, introduced his ball-control passing game and led the Redskins to the NFL championship in the franchise's first Washington season (after a move from Boston) while touching off a remarkable 16-year career that would produce five division titles, another championship and 16 major records.

Baugh is remembered as the man who revolutionized the offensive concept of the game. He spent the first half of his career as a triple-threat halfback in the Redskins' single-wing offense and the second half as an All-Pro quarterback in the new T-formation. Opponents marveled at the whip-like motion Baugh used to deliver bullet passes in a pass-only-in-desperation era. Form meant nothing to the Redskins' quiet man, who delivered the ball underhanded, from the ear, sidearm, off-balance, hard, soft or in any other manner that would get his team to the end zone.

BEST PLAYERS I'VE SEEN

SELECTED BY MIKE DITKA

1. Walter Payton	6. Johnny Unitas
2. Jerry Rice	7. Dick Butkus
3. Joe Montana	8. Ray Nitschke
4. John Elway	9. Sammy Baugh
5. Dan Marino	10. Don Hutson

But offense was only half the Baugh story. He doubled in his first seven seasons as an outstanding defensive back who once intercepted a record four passes in a game. He also was an outstanding quick-kicker and punter who still owns records for career (45.1 yards per kick) and season average (51.4). When Baugh retired as a four-time NFL passing-yardage leader, he had thrown for a then-amazing 21,886 yards and completed 56.5 percent of his passes for a record 187 touchdowns.

12

BARRY SANDERS

He's a human light show, a jumping, bounding, now-you-see-him, now-you-don't beam that appears and vanishes at the blink of an eye. The Detroit Lions' Barry Sanders, all 5-8, 203 pounds of him, is oozing with the light-flashing quickness that former teammate Chris Spielman says "can flat-out embarrass anyone."

Every run is filled with stops, starts, jukes, head fakes, cuts, changes of direction and broken tackles that electrify fans, whether it nets one yard or 90.

The quickness comes from powerful legs and uncanny balance, a combination that allows Sanders to change course with smooth, quick and decisive moves. Defenders who underestimate Sanders' legs are left flailing in his wake. Sanders also has great leaping ability and superior speed, but his ability to back out of a closing hole with dazzling, impossible spins is what sets him apart.

The former Heisman Trophy winner from Oklahoma State, who was deemed too small to make a big impact when he was drafted third overall in 1989, immediately became a yardage machine. Operating in the Lions' one-back set as a rookie, he exploded into prominence with 1,470 rushing yards, the first of a record-setting 10 straight seasons in which he has topped the 1,000-yard plateau. When the offense changed in 1997, Sanders followed his fullback for 2,053 yards, the third 2,000-yard season in NFL history, and tacked on 305 yards with 33 receptions.

Quiet, shy and introspective off the field, Sanders is flashy and aggressive with a football in his hands. The common personality denominator is dependability, which is reflected in his 15,269 yards and No. 2 ranking on the career rushing list entering the 1999 season—only 1,457 behind all-time leader Walter Payton. The 10-time Pro Bowl selection has rushed for 99 career touchdowns, even though he often has been removed for a power back in goal-line situations, but has not been able to get the Lions to a Super Bowl.

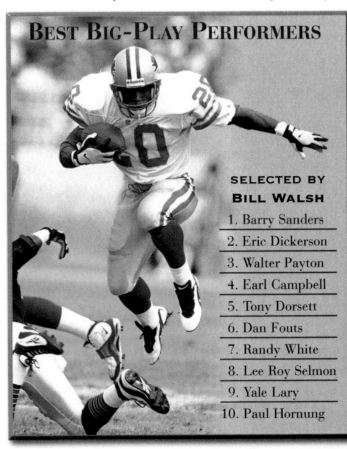

BEST BIG-PLAY PERFORMERS

SELECTED BY BILL WALSH

1. Barry Sanders
2. Eric Dickerson
3. Walter Payton
4. Earl Campbell
5. Tony Dorsett
6. Dan Fouts
7. Randy White
8. Lee Roy Selmon
9. Yale Lary
10. Paul Hornung

"HE MAKES YOU STAND
ON YOUR TOES ANY TIME
HE GETS THE BALL.
YOU WATCH BECAUSE YOU
FEEL SOMETHING BIG'S
ABOUT TO HAPPEN."

FORMER LIONS COACH
WAYNE FONTES, 1990
TSN PRO FOOTBALL
YEARBOOK

13

DEACON JONES

T rying to ignore Deacon Jones was like trying to ignore a parade through your living room. He was colorful, cocky, confident—and athletically gifted, the leader of the Los Angeles Rams' Fearsome

Foursome defensive line in the 1960s. Jones was a fast, rugged and mobile sackmaster, a Gino Marchetti-like pass rusher who helped set the standard for modern defensive end play.

Jones was a 6-5, 272-pound unknown when he was selected out of Mississippi Valley State in the 14th round of the 1961 NFL draft. But that changed quickly. Jones played with the same flamboyant personality that he exhibited with reporters and soon became the leader of a devastating line that also included tackles Merlin Olsen and Roosevelt Grier and end Lamar Lundy.

Deacon (a self-ascribed moniker that replaced the "too common" David) became a terror for blockers who were not quick enough to keep him from bursting into the backfield and quarterbacks who had to scramble for their lives. It was Jones who coined the term sack,

TOUGHEST DEFENSIVE ENDS
SELECTED BY ART SHELL

1. Deacon Jones	6. Aaron Brown
2. Lyle Alzado	7. Cedrick Hardman
3. Elvin Bethea	8. L.C. Greenwood
4. Fred Dean	9. Coy Bacon
5. Rich Jackson	10. Bill Stanfill

"You know, like you sack a city—you devastate it." In an effort to control Jones, teams used double- and triple-teams, but that strategy simply freed Olsen, his partner in the best tackle/end combination in NFL history.

Jones' greatest asset was the sprinter-like speed that allowed him to roam from sideline-to-sideline, delivering what he called "civilized violence." A departure from the stay-at-home defensive linemen of his era, Jones also popularized the head slap, a maneuver that later was outlawed by the NFL. Over a 14-year career that included brief stops in San Diego and Washington, Jones earned five consensus All-Pro citations and played in eight Pro Bowls. He never played in an NFL championship game or a Super Bowl.

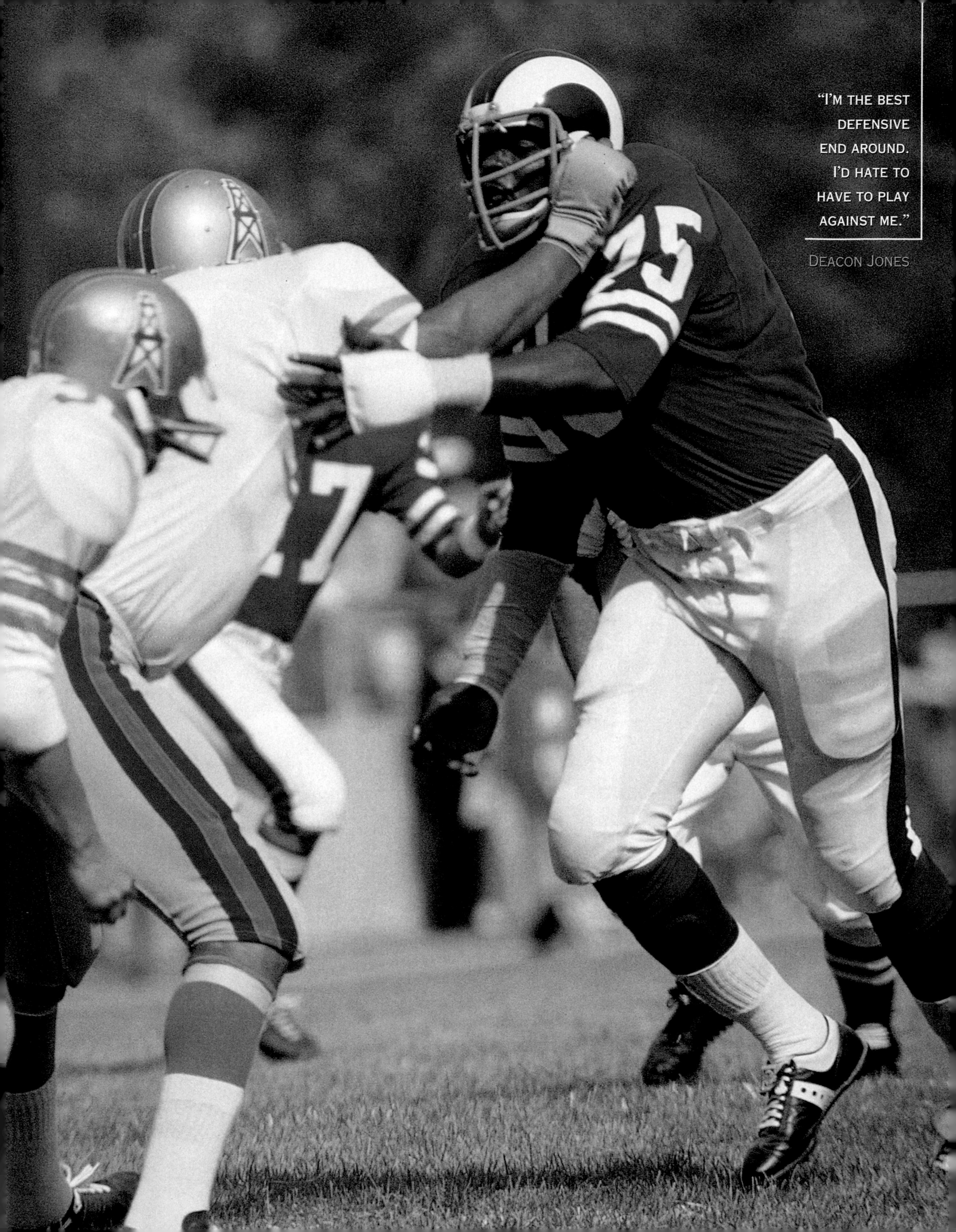

"I'M THE BEST DEFENSIVE END AROUND. I'D HATE TO HAVE TO PLAY AGAINST ME."

DEACON JONES

"HE'S THE BEST I'VE SEEN. HE SET THE STANDARD FOR US. PHYSICALLY, HE HAD ALL THE NECESSARY ATTRIBUTES BUT HE ALSO SET THE STANDARD FOR ATTITUDE. THERE WILL NEVER BE ANOTHER JOE GREENE. JOE WILL ALWAYS BE SOMETHING SPECIAL."

FORMER STEELERS COACH CHUCK NOLL

14

JOE GREENE

I f the bear-paw hands couldn't twist a blocker into submission, the club-like forearms might finish the job. The heads of many NFL offensive linemen were sent into a throbbing spin by bell-ringing blows to the helmet from

Joe Greene. He was the meanest, nastiest, most ornery member of Pittsburgh's Steel Curtain defense and the cornerstone upon which a four-time Super Bowl champion was built.

The 6-4, 275-pound Greene could single-handedly dominate a game. He was strong, mobile and hostile—a grizzly bear looking for a quarterback snack. Mean Joe didn't just overpower blockers, he brutalized them with a no-holds-barred style. He was cocky enough to believe he could do anything he wanted any time he wanted to—and he usually did, double- and triple-team blocking notwithstanding.

Like in the December 10, 1972, game against Houston when Greene recorded five sacks, blocked a field-goal attempt, forced a fumble and recovered a fumble in a 9-3 victory that helped the Steelers secure the first of their seven AFC Central titles in the 1970s. Off the field, Greene was articulate, outspoken, thoughtful and quick to smile. On the field, he was on a mission of destruction, the anchor for a run-stuffing wall that included L.C. Greenwood, Ernie Holmes and Dwight White.

Times were tough in Pittsburgh when Greene, out of North Texas State, was selected in the first round (fourth overall) in 1969—the first pick of the Chuck

Noll coaching era. But with the man who would come to epitomize Pittsburgh-style football stationed on the line, the Steelers rose to prominence, ending almost four decades of frustration by reaching the

BEST PLAYERS I'VE SEEN
SELECTED BY JACK HAM

1. Jim Brown
2. Roger Staubach
3. Walter Payton
4. Gale Sayers
5. Anthony Munoz
6. O.J. Simpson
7. Joe Greene
8. Kellen Winslow
9. Dan Marino
10. Andy Russell

AFC championship game six times in eight years and winning four Super Bowls in six years. Greene's relentless pursuit of excellence was reflected in 10 Pro Bowl selections in a 13-year career that ended in 1981.

15

GINO MARCHETTI

Call him the dominator, the intimidator, the terminator. Gino Marchetti was all that and more. He was to the defensive end position what Sammy Baugh was to quarterback, Don Hutson to wide receiver and Lawrence Taylor to outside linebacker. He was the prototype, the standard by which future generations of defensive ends would be judged.

Marchetti combined size (6-4, 244), agility and

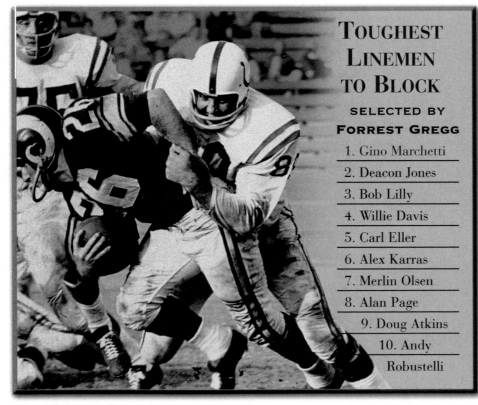

TOUGHEST LINEMEN TO BLOCK

SELECTED BY
FORREST GREGG

1. Gino Marchetti
2. Deacon Jones
3. Bob Lilly
4. Willie Davis
5. Carl Eller
6. Alex Karras
7. Merlin Olsen
8. Alan Page
9. Doug Atkins
10. Andy Robustelli

pressuring the quarterback—a function he performed with an almost demonic fervor.

Marchetti was big and fast enough to overpower anybody who blocked his path to the quarterback. His relentless charges were executed with a wild passion that spread fear throughout the league, and his explosiveness off the snap confounded double- and triple-team blocking tactics. Trying to block Marchetti was like trying to stop a steamroller moving at warp speed. He simply overwhelmed some of the best tackles in the game.

Marchetti's menacing aura was enhanced by the dark-bearded jaws and piercing eyes that flashed at offensive linemen from inside his helmet. And his legend grew with stories of how he had played half of one game with a separated shoulder and another game two weeks after undergoing surgery for an appendicitis.

amazing big-man quickness in his 13-year role as the Baltimore Colts' chief run-stuffer and pass rusher. He became the first defensive end specialist in the early 1950s, when coaches were phasing out two-way players. And he introduced the concept of an end

At 18, Marchetti fought in the Battle of the Bulge during World War II. He then attended the University of San Francisco, helped the Colts capture two NFL championships, played in 10 Pro Bowls and earned All-Pro honors every year from 1956 to '62.

"HE'S THE
GREATEST PLAYER
IN FOOTBALL.
IT'S A WASTE
OF TIME
TO RUN AROUND
THIS GUY'S END.
IT'S A LOST PLAY.
YOU DON'T
BOTHER
TO TRY IT."

FORMER
RAMS COACH
SID GILLMAN,
1959

"HE'S MOST DANGEROUS BECAUSE HE HAS THE ABILITY TO RUN TO HIS LEFT AND THROW THE BALL BACK TO HIS RIGHT WITH A LOT OF MUSTARD ON IT. WHEN HE'S RUNNING TO HIS RIGHT, HE CAN THROW IT 60 YARDS ON ONE FOOT."

FORMER RAIDERS CORNERBACK
MIKE HAYNES, 1986
THE SPORTING NEWS

16

JOHN ELWAY

It starts with the arm, that magnificent right arm that delivered passes long, short, from impossible angles, off the wrong foot and while he was lying down, falling down, kneeling and running left or right. It was unfailingly

dependable for 16 NFL seasons, the scourge of defensive backs and the architect of numerous magic moments. It was the go-to weapon in a sizable arsenal, the one that most likely would fire when everything was on the line.

It seemed to be that way forever, from John Elway's early days as a record-setting Stanford quarterback to his selection as the No. 1 overall draft pick of 1983 and his career as the unflappable field general of the Denver Broncos. The arm was good enough to earn him a minor league contract with the New York Yankees and to break the hearts of Cleveland Browns fans in the 1986 postseason with The Drive, the 98-yard march that epitomized Elway's reputation as one of the greatest comeback quarterbacks of all time. Elway's other skills were overshadowed but no less feared.

BEST PLAYERS I'VE SEEN
SELECTED BY WILLIE BROWN

1. Jim Brown	6. Lawrence Taylor
2. John Elway	7. Ted Hendricks
3. Jerry Rice	8. Jim Parker
4. O.J. Simpson	9. Paul Warfield
5. Joe Namath	10. Joe Greene

He lulled opponents to sleep with that blond, blue-eyed All-American boy look, his big, white teeth permanently displayed by a fixed half-smile. Then he would run them ragged as he scrambled away from danger, his quick feet gaining valuable time for receivers to get open. The physical skills were complemented by a great understanding of his offense, a commanding field presence and a competitive fire that burned hottest when a game was on the line.

Elway finished the 1998 season ranked second all time in passing yards (51,475) and third in touchdown passes (300), but his career probably will be measured more by the consecutive Super Bowl wins he delivered after the 1997 and 1998 seasons. A nine-time Pro Bowl selection, Elway also pushed three less-talented Broncos teams to Super Bowl appearances that ended in one-sided defeats.

17

ANTHONY MUNOZ

He was a human avalanche, 278 pounds of beef caving in on a helpless defender. When Anthony Munoz attacked, the physical onslaught continued until somebody was on the ground.

The Cincinnati Bengals' Raging Bull snorted and pawed his way through the NFL for 13 outstanding seasons, drawing near-universal praise as the best offensive tackle in the game's history.

The 6-6, 278-pound former USC star was an intimidating physical presence. But his powerful body also moved around the field with surprising quickness and agility. "His head alone weighs 200 pounds," marveled one scout on draft day in 1980, but the secret to Munoz's success was the huge legs that gave him the leverage to move any defensive end he might face. He played offense with the attack mentality of a defender.

Not surprisingly, the Bengals directed their power running attack over tackle and Munoz helped clear a path to Super Bowl appearances after the 1981 and 1988 seasons—both of which ended in close losses to the San Francisco 49ers. Finesse was not part of his game, whether driving defenders 10 yards off the line or protecting quarterbacks Ken Anderson and Boomer Esiason from evil-minded rushers. Munoz's quickness,

toughness and consistency impressed coaches, teammates and opponents, earning him 11 straight Pro Bowl invitations and gushing testimonials.

The ferocious dedication he exhibited on the field

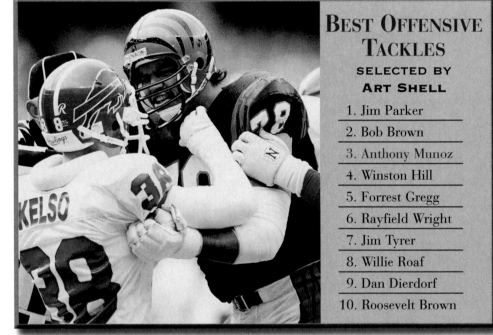

BEST OFFENSIVE TACKLES
SELECTED BY ART SHELL

1. Jim Parker
2. Bob Brown
3. Anthony Munoz
4. Winston Hill
5. Forrest Gregg
6. Rayfield Wright
7. Jim Tyrer
8. Willie Roaf
9. Dan Dierdorf
10. Roosevelt Brown

was contrasted by the quiet, polite, unassuming personality that won him friends and praise throughout the Cincinnati community. When he won the NFL's prestigious Man of the Year award in 1991, a smile lit up his normally scowling face. When he retired after the 1992 season, a different kind of a smile could be seen on the faces of most defensive coordinators, who had never seen the charitable side of Munoz.

"Anthony Munoz was the epitome of what an NFL offensive lineman should be. I've never seen one better."

Hall of Fame tackle
Mike McCormack

18

RAY NITSCHKE

Forget the rumors: Ray Nitschke never ate barbed wire or spit nails. But he could take responsibility for many of the other legendary stories that circulated through the NFL during his 15-year journey to the Hall of Fame. Nitschke's true legacy is intertwined with Vince Lombardi's Green Bay Packers, a team that fed off Nitschke's fierce determination to capture five NFL championships over a seven-year period in the 1960s.

Off the field, Nitschke was a tall, balding,

"IT'S NOT SO MUCH HIS SPEED OR EVEN HIS QUICKNESS.
IT'S HIS DESIRE TO MAKE THE PLAY, AN ABILITY TO GET
TO THE RIGHT SPOT AHEAD OF EVERYBODY ELSE. HE HAS
ALL THE STRENGTH AND TOUGHNESS NEEDED TO BE TRULY
OUTSTANDING AND, AS A LEADER, HE IS WITHOUT PEER."

FORMER RAMS LINEBACKER LES RICHTER

intelligent, thoughtful and conservative businessman, complete with horn-rimmed glasses and traditional suit. But once he pulled a helmet over the bald head and removed his upper bridge, he became a ferocious, body-slamming middle linebacker. The 6-3, 235-pound Nitschke who entertained rabid Green Bay fans on Sunday afternoons had the strength, quickness, lateral speed and toughness to back up the toothless, animalistic aura he used to intimidate opponents.

To say he was the heart of the Packers' defense during the team's glory years is an understatement. Nitschke inspired greatness in teammates with his all-out, never-say-die hustle, a never-wavering enthusiasm and a leader-by-example mentality. He played mean and his reputation as one of the greatest run-stuffing linebackers was well deserved. He also was a cat-like pass defender who rattled receivers and ran back 25 interceptions for 385 yards.

The image of a scowling Nitschke, with blood-spattered on his No. 66 uniform and white tape wrapped tightly around various parts of his body to hide and protect his numerous injuries, will live long in Green Bay football lore. Curiously, he was selected for only one Pro Bowl during his outstanding career. But he was named a linebacker on the NFL's 75th anniversary all-time team that was selected in 1994.

FEARED DEFENDERS OVER THE MIDDLE
SELECTED BY CHARLEY TAYLOR

1. Ray Nitschke	6. Chuck Howley
2. Dick Butkus	7. Maxie Baughan
3. Mike Singletary	8. Cornell Green
4. Willie Lanier	9. Cliff Harris
5. Jack Ham	

19 NIGHT TRAIN LANE

"TRAIN WILL ALWAYS BE THE GODFATHER
OF CORNERBACKS. HE WAS AS LARGE
AS SOME LINEMEN OF HIS ERA.
HE ALSO WAS AGILE AND VERY FAST.
HIS TACKLING WAS AWESOME. HE DID THE
CLOTHESLINE AND OTHER TACKLES THAT
JUST DEVASTATED THE BALLCARRIER."

LEM BARNEY, 1999

Former Green Bay coach Vince Lombardi called him the greatest cornerback he had ever seen. NFL wide receivers who carried battle scars from his vicious hits called him mean and uncompromising.

Love him or hate him, Dick "Night Train" Lane was a defensive force, a fearless ballhawk who disrupted passing attacks for 14 outstanding seasons with the Los Angeles Rams, Chicago Cardinals and Detroit Lions.

Incredibly, the 6-1, 194-pound Lane had never played above the junior college level when he showed up at the Rams' offices in 1952 and asked for a tryout. Soon he was getting on-the-job training against some of the NFL's best receivers in one-on-one situations. His instincts were sharp, his athleticism good enough to make up for the inevitable mistakes. When Lane's rookie season ended, he had 14 interceptions—a still-standing NFL record—and a pair of touchdown returns.

The flamboyant Night Train, who got his nickname from a popular musical recording of his era, defined how to play cornerback, experimenting and learning as he went along. Lane developed the reputation as a mean-spirited headhunter, who would bring down ballcarriers with clothesline and facemask tackles that prompted legislation to outlaw such tactics. Many receivers, understandably wary, were defeated before the ball was ever snapped.

Lane was an impact player who made good things happen, primarily with his big-play, gambling style and a fierce determination to win. He was one of the NFL's original ball-strippers and his reputation for dishing out pain was almost legendary. Happy and fun-loving off the field, he played with an edge that few could match. When he finished his career in 1965 after six years with the Lions, he had 68 interceptions, a figure that still ranks third on the all-time list.

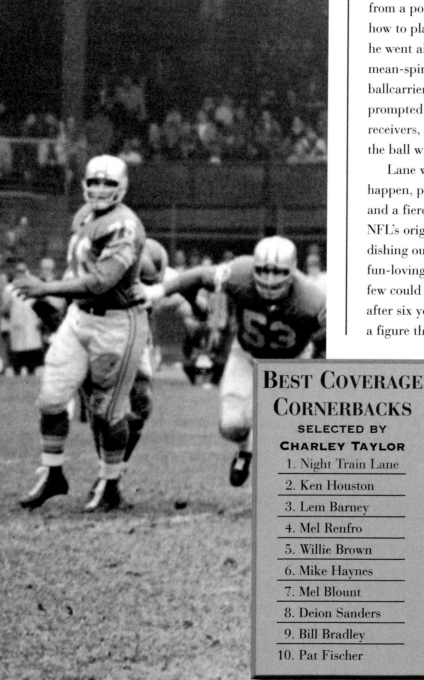

BEST COVERAGE CORNERBACKS
SELECTED BY
CHARLEY TAYLOR

1. Night Train Lane
2. Ken Houston
3. Lem Barney
4. Mel Renfro
5. Willie Brown
6. Mike Haynes
7. Mel Blount
8. Deion Sanders
9. Bill Bradley
10. Pat Fischer

20

JOHN HANNAH

Intense. Physical. Intimidating. Relentless. Tough. Adjectives roll off the tongue like defensive linemen used to roll off the powerful body of New England Patriots guard John Hannah. He was a legend in the football

trenches, a grunt-and-groan trailblazer for 13 NFL seasons. When the Patriots needed a tough yard, Hannah made sure they got it.

The 6-2, 265-pound former Alabama star was the outstanding run-blocker of his era. Defensive players who did not have their helmet strapped on tight were in danger of losing it with one of his trademark forearm blows. Hannah intimidated quietly and dominated thoroughly, operating with a ruthless, business-like efficiency on every play. He was frightening when he pulled on sweeps or other power runs, a nightmare for defensive ends and linebackers who were daring enough to step into his path.

Hannah's quickness and physical game were impressive, but no more than the intensity he put into preparation for every game. He knew the strengths and weaknesses of every opponent and entered every contest with a personal game plan. Hannah's strength was execution and he approached every play as if it would be his last. When he stepped up to the line with eyes ablaze, nobody doubted who was in control.

Not surprisingly, the Patriots thrived with Hannah patrolling the middle of their power running attack. They rushed for a season-record 3,165 yards in 1978 and won an AFC championship in 1985 before losing to the powerful Chicago Bears in Super

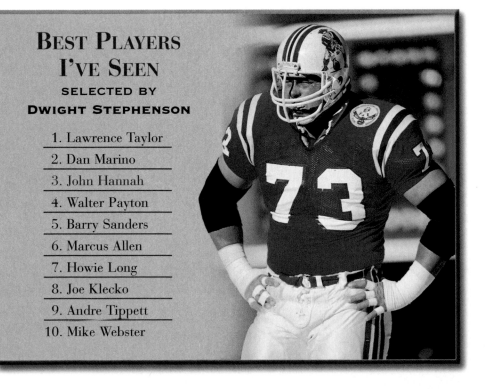

BEST PLAYERS I'VE SEEN
SELECTED BY
DWIGHT STEPHENSON

1. Lawrence Taylor
2. Dan Marino
3. John Hannah
4. Walter Payton
5. Barry Sanders
6. Marcus Allen
7. Howie Long
8. Joe Klecko
9. Andre Tippett
10. Mike Webster

Bowl XX. Hannah, the son of former NFL lineman Herb Hannah and the brother of former NFL lineman Charley Hannah, retired after his lone Super Bowl appearance. He was a nine-time Pro Bowl selection.

"YOU NEVER HAVE TO GRADE
JOHN BECAUSE YOU KNOW WHAT
HE IS DOING IN EVERY GAME—
PLAYING HIS GUTS OUT.
WHEN THE GAME IS OVER,
HE HAS NOTHING LEFT."

FORMER PATRIOTS COACH
RAYMOND BERRY

21 GALE SAYERS

Catching up with Gale Sayers was a 60-minute task. If he didn't burn you with one of his gliding, stutter-stepping bursts up the middle, he probably would get you with a reception, a halfback pass or an electrifying return. He was lightning just waiting to strike, an offensive weapon just waiting to be unleashed. If Sayers wasn't the most prolific all-around performer in NFL history, he probably ran a close second.

It all started with his powerful legs. He could hit the hole in a blink with his long, low stride, then sidestep traffic and accelerate to daylight. The 6-0, 198-pound Sayers was a master at reversing directions or wiggling and squirming his way through a swarm of tacklers. He seemed to have a variety of gears. Just when a tackler thought Sayers was going full speed, he could turn it up a notch and explode into the open.

Sayers became the most celebrated newcomer in NFL history when he scored a rookie-record 22 touchdowns in 1965—14 on the ground, six via the pass, one on a kickoff return and one on a punt return. Included in that total were the six TDs he scored in a memorable game against San Francisco—four on runs, one on an 80-yard pass and one on an 85-yard punt return. He followed that by rushing for 1,231 yards in his second season, winning his first of two rushing titles.

But the magic would end after a much-too-short 68-game career, thanks to a series of knee injuries. The quiet, self-confident Sayers played his final two games in 1971 at age 28; his knees wouldn't take any more punishment and Chicago mourned. He finished with incredible averages of 5.0 yards per run, 11.7 per catch, 30.6 per kickoff return and 14.5 per punt return. He was named the top player in three of his four Pro Bowl appearances, but he never played in a postseason game.

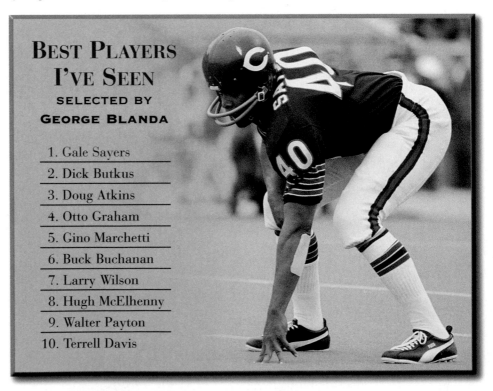

BEST PLAYERS I'VE SEEN
SELECTED BY
GEORGE BLANDA

1. Gale Sayers
2. Dick Butkus
3. Doug Atkins
4. Otto Graham
5. Gino Marchetti
6. Buck Buchanan
7. Larry Wilson
8. Hugh McElhenny
9. Walter Payton
10. Terrell Davis

"SAYERS IS THE GREATEST PLAYER I'VE EVER SEEN.
THAT'S RIGHT—THE GREATEST. I'VE NEVER BEEN
MORE IMPRESSED WITH ONE PLAYER."

DICK BUTKUS, 1965
THE SPORTING NEWS

22
REGGIE WHITE

The head-ringing blows he delivered on a football field stood in stark contrast to the messages of love and understanding he preached from a pulpit. Reggie White was a contradiction in cleats, a 290-pound champion of peace and dispenser of controlled violence. Over a 15-year professional career that started in 1984 with the Memphis Showboats in the USFL and continued with the Philadelphia Eagles and Green Bay Packers, he handled both roles with vigor and passion, a tribute to his dual commitment as a licensed Baptist minister and football's "Minister of Defense."

His football passion was driven by a powerful body that could stampede blockers and move around the field with catlike quickness and sprinter's speed. The sight of the hulking White glaring at a quarterback from his defensive end position was enough to disrupt game plans and trigger premature exits from the pocket. He was the focus of pregame meetings, the defender who could dictate offensive strategy and turn games by himself. His durability also was special. In 1985, in fact, he played in a combined 31 games (18 with Memphis and 13 with Philadelphia).

White's unyielding desire was to get to the quarterback, a goal he achieved 192½ times—more sacks than any player in history. Off the field, he was a humanitarian, a community servant and street-corner champion of the oppressed. On the field, he was a relentless quarterback chaser and run-stuffer no one

player could block. White's 21 sacks for the Eagles in 1987 fell one short of Mark Gastineau's all-time record—and he did it in 12 games during a strike-shortened season.

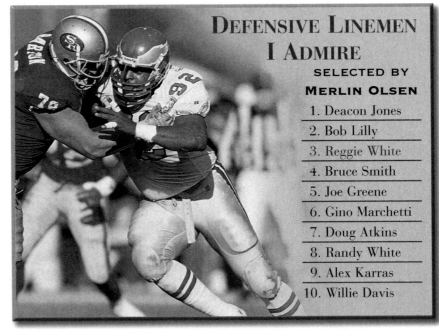

DEFENSIVE LINEMEN I ADMIRE
SELECTED BY
MERLIN OLSEN

1. Deacon Jones
2. Bob Lilly
3. Reggie White
4. Bruce Smith
5. Joe Greene
6. Gino Marchetti
7. Doug Atkins
8. Randy White
9. Alex Karras
10. Willie Davis

It's no coincidence the Packers regained long-lost prominence in 1993, the year White ended his eight-season tenure in Philadelphia by signing a free-agent contract. The Pack reached the playoffs in each of White's six Green Bay seasons and captured a Super Bowl—their first in 29 years—after the 1996 campaign. And it's no coincidence that before White retired after the '98 season, he earned an impressive 13 Pro Bowl selections.

"He's the best
I've ever seen.
The size, the strength,
the speed. He's got
everything. He never
lets up, either. That's the
thing; he's relentless."

Eagles defensive lineman
Mike Pitts, 1988
TSN Pro Football Yearbook

23
RONNIE LOTT

"HE WAS ONE OF THE BEST SAFETIES EVER TO PLAY THE GAME. HE HAD IT ALL. HE WAS AS SMART AS EMLEN TUNNELL, A GREAT HITTER AND A GREAT COVER GUY. HE DID EVERYTHING."

RAYMOND BERRY, 1999

The footsteps wide receivers often heard in their worst nightmares belonged to Ronnie Lott, who left a black-and-blue imprint on the NFL over an outstanding 14-season career. He was the last line of defense, an enforcer who had to make every hit count. Nobody did that better than Lott and nobody who ventured into his area of concern escaped without paying a stiff price.

Nothing personal, but the talented cornerback-turned-safety took his job seriously. Lott was competitive and resourceful and his never-give-an-inch style helped inspire the 49ers to four Super Bowl championships. He was a throwback, a ballhawking defender who threw his 6-foot, 203-pound body around like a middle linebacker.

Though it seemed as though Lott played with reckless abandon, his style was actually crafted out of his amazing sense and feel for what was about to happen on every play. Any quarterback who threw a ball into the secondary did so with full knowledge that Lott would be ready to pounce.

Every receiver who reached for a pass did so in fear of a torpedo-like shot to the ribs. He was successful as a cornerback early in his career, but his reputation grew with the 1985 move to free safety and a later shift to strong safety.

Lott, a former USC star who was as gentle and soft-spoken off the field as he was intimidating on it, completed his career in 1994 after 10 seasons with the 49ers and two-year stints with the Los Angeles Raiders and New York Jets. He finished with 63 interceptions, good for fifth place on the all-time list. He also finished with 10 Pro Bowl selections and recognition as one of the best safeties ever to play the game.

BEST DEFENDERS I'VE FACED
SELECTED BY TROY AIKMAN

1. Lawrence Taylor	6. Ronnie Lott
2. Reggie White	7. Tim McDonald
3. Bruce Smith	8. Merton Hanks
4. Howie Long	9. Bryant Young
5. Carl Banks	10. Aeneas Williams

24 JIM PARKER

"I LOVED PLAYING NEXT TO
JIM. HE WAS THE BEST, MAN.
HE PLAYED EVERY POSITION
ALONG THE LINE AND WAS
GREAT AT ALL OF THEM.
HE WAS ONE OF THOSE GUYS
WHO JUST PUNISHED YOU.
HE SMOTHERED YOU."

JOHN MACKEY, 1999

The straightest path to Johnny Unitas made a half-circle detour around left tackle. Big Jim Parker wouldn't have it any other way. He was the quarterback's blindside protector, the man entrusted with the continued good health and welfare of Baltimore's most valuable property. And he diligently made sure that nobody violated that trust for 11 outstanding NFL seasons.

Parker is considered by many historians the greatest offensive tackle in pro football history—and the greatest guard. He spent his first 5½ seasons working over the league's big and fast defensive ends and the next 5½ at guard, where his blocking responsibilities changed considerably. It didn't seem to matter. Parker was a Pro Bowl regular from 1959 to '66 and a Hall of Famer in the making no matter where the Colts chose to position him.

The 6-3, 273-pound former Ohio State star not only was one of the biggest linemen of his day, he was the fastest big man. He was like a human avalanche when he exploded off the line on a straight running play and a relentless bulldozer when he cleared traffic on power sweeps, which came all too often for opposing linebackers and defensive backs. But Parker was at his best as an impenetrable pass-blocker. His massive body, great balance, quick feet and superior blocking technique held back all rushers, the more the merrier.

It's not surprising that Parker's arrival coincided

BEST PLAYERS I'VE SEEN

SELECTED BY
WILLIE LANIER

1. Lenny Moore
2. Johnny Unitas
3. Jim Brown
4. Jim Parker
5. Raymond Berry
6. Walter Payton
7. Barry Sanders
8. Deion Sanders
9. Jerry Rice
10. Steve Young

with the Colts' rise to prominence in the 1950s. They won consecutive NFL championships in 1958 and 1959 and regrouped after a four-year falloff to reach the league title game in 1964. Conscientious, hard-working and durable (he didn't miss a game over his first 10 pro seasons), Parker became the model that young offensive linemen studied to learn their craft.

"MERLIN DIDN'T TALK MUCH.
HE PROBABLY WAS THE BEST
OF THE RAMS' FRONT FOUR.
HE WOULD CHASE YOU FROM
HERE TO GEORGIA JUST TO
BEAT YOU. HE WAS THE KEY
TO THE FOURSOME."

HALL OF FAME
OFFENSIVE LINEMAN
JIM PARKER, 1999

25

MERLIN OLSEN

Watching Merlin Olsen play football was like watching a surgeon in an operating room. No wasted motion, precise and near-perfect technique, absolute confidence and self-control.

Olsen performed his operations on Sunday afternoons for 15 NFL seasons, carving up linemen and quarterbacks who struggled to deal with one of the greatest defensive lines ever assembled.

As the stabilizing force and charter member of the Los Angeles Rams' Fearsome Foursome defensive front wall in the 1960s, the 6-5, 270-pound Olsen was a prototypical tackle with incredible upper body strength, explosive speed and the agility to outmaneuver frustrated blockers. But the real secret to his success came from within—the Phi Beta Kappa classroom skills that he used to dissect the game and the players he competed against.

Off the field, Olsen was a gentle giant who spoke with soft, measured words about topics ranging from finance to politics. On the field, he played with control and discipline, unwilling to get caught up in the emotion and animalistic violence that sometimes dominated his occupation. He worked for 10 years as the left-side partner with Hall of Fame end Deacon Jones, forming one of the great pass-rushing, run-stuffing combinations in NFL history.

Jones was the speed-rushing, colorful playmaker. Olsen was the quiet, steady practitioner who stayed at

home and covered up for his partner. The Rams' linemen worked innovative stunting and looping maneuvers that had never been tried before, many

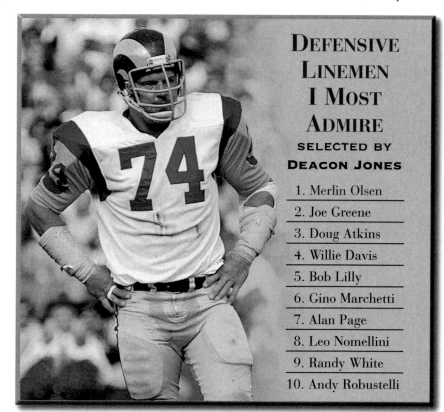

DEFENSIVE LINEMEN I MOST ADMIRE

SELECTED BY DEACON JONES

1. Merlin Olsen
2. Joe Greene
3. Doug Atkins
4. Willie Davis
5. Bob Lilly
6. Gino Marchetti
7. Alan Page
8. Leo Nomellini
9. Randy White
10. Andy Robustelli

conceived by the analytical Olsen. A first-round pick in 1962 from Utah State, Olsen became a starter in the third game of his rookie season and played in 208 regular-season games, the final 198 in succession. He never played in an NFL championship game or Super Bowl, but before he retired in 1976, he earned a record 14 straight Pro Bowl invitations.

	1920-29	1930-39	1940-49	1950-59	1960-69

Player	Rank	From	To
Jim Thorpe	(88)	1920	1928
Red Grange	(80)	1925	1934
Bronko Nagurski	(35)	1930	1943
Mel Hein	(74)	1931	1945
Don Hutson	(6)	1935	1945
Sammy Baugh	(11)	1937	1952
Sid Luckman	(39)	1939	1950
Steve Van Buren	(77)	1944	1951
Otto Graham	(7)	1946	1955
Marion Motley	(32)	1946	1955
Elroy Hirsch	(89)	1946	1957
Lou Groza	(99)	1946	1967
Emlen Tunnell	(70)	1948	1961
Bobby Layne	(52)	1948	1962
Chuck Bednarik	(54)	1949	1962
George Blanda	(98)	1949	1975
Jack Christiansen	(86)	1951	1958
Night Train Lane	(19)	1952	1965
Bill George	(49)	1952	1966
Gino Marchetti	(15)	1952	1966
Roosevelt Brown	(57)	1953	1965
Joe Schmidt	(65)	1953	1965
Raymond Berry	(40)	1955	1967
Lenny Moore	(71)	1956	1967
Sam Huff	(76)	1956	1969
Forrest Gregg	(28)	1956	1971
Bart Starr	(41)	1956	1971
Johnny Unitas	(5)	1956	1973
Jim Brown	(1)	1957	1965
Jim Parker	(24)	1957	1967
Willie Davis	(69)	1958	1969
Ray Nitschke	(18)	1958	1972
Larry Wilson	(43)	1960	1972
Jim Otto	(78)	1960	1974
Herb Adderley	(45)	1961	1972
Mike Ditka	(90)	1961	1972
Deacon Jones	(13)	1961	1974
Bob Lilly	(10)	1961	1974
Fran Tarkenton	(59)	1961	1978
Lance Alworth	(31)	1962	1972
Merlin Olsen	(25)	1962	1976
John Mackey	(48)	1963	1972
Bobby Bell	(66)	1963	1974
Buck Buchanan	(67)	1963	1975
Willie Brown	(50)	1963	1978
Charley Taylor	(85)	1964	1977
Paul Warfield	(60)	1964	1977
Gale Sayers	(21)	1965	1971
Dick Butkus	(9)	1965	1973
Joe Namath	(96)	1965	1977
Fred Biletnikoff	(94)	1965	1978
Lem Barney	(97)	1967	1977
Willie Lanier	(42)	1967	1977
Ken Houston	(61)	1967	1980
Larry Little	(79)	1967	1980
Alan Page	(34)	1967	1981
Gene Upshaw	(62)	1967	1981
Art Shell	(55)	1968	1982
O.J. Simpson	(26)	1969	1979
Roger Staubach	(29)	1969	1979
Joe Greene	(14)	1969	1981
Ted Hendricks	(64)	1969	1983
Charlie Joiner	(100)	1969	1986
Mel Blount	(36)	1970	1983
Terry Bradshaw	(44)	1970	1983
Jack Ham	(47)	1971	1982
Franco Harris	(83)	1972	1984
John Hannah	(20)	1973	1985
Dan Fouts	(92)	1973	1987
Jack Lambert	(30)	1974	1984
Mike Webster	(75)	1974	1990
Walter Payton	(8)	1975	1987
Randy White	(51)	1975	1988
Mike Haynes	(93)	1976	1989
Steve Largent	(46)	1976	1989
Tony Dorsett	(53)	1977	1988
Earl Campbell	(33)	1978	1985
Kellen Winslow	(73)	1979	1987
Joe Montana	(3)	1979	1994
Dwight Stephenson	(84)	1980	1987
Anthony Munoz	(17)	1980	1992
Art Monk	(91)	1980	1995
Mike Singletary	(56)	1981	1992
Lawrence Taylor	(4)	1981	1993
Ronnie Lott	(23)	1981	1994
Marcus Allen	(72)	1982	1997
Eric Dickerson	(38)	1983	1993
John Elway	(16)	1983	1998
Darrell Green	(81)	1983	1998
Dan Marino	(27)	1983	1998
Jerry Rice	(2)	1985	1998
Bruce Smith	(58)	1985	1998
Reggie White	(22)	1985	1998
Steve Young	(63)	1985	1998
Rod Woodson	(87)	1987	1998
Troy Aikman	(95)	1989	1998
Barry Sanders	(12)	1989	1998
Deion Sanders	(37)	1989	1998
Emmitt Smith	(68)	1990	1998
Brett Favre	(82)	1991	1998

Active players each year: 1 1 1 1 1 1 2 1 1 1 1 2 3 3 3 3 3 3 4 3 4 4 4 4 4 4 5 5 5 7 7 9 11 11 13 14 13 15 18 19 21 19 21 27 28 30 32 35 32 36 32 38

RONNIE LOTT

GEORGE HALAS (LEFT) AND SID LUCKMAN, 1940

JACK LAMBERT

TIMELINE

A chronological breakdown of the Top 100 in professional football, accompanied by an alphabetical listing and a yearly total of active players. The breakdown begins with the first season (1920) of the NFL and includes seasons played in the All-America Football Conference from 1946-49 and the American Football League from 1960-69.

Chronological Listing

Player	Rank	From	To
Jim Thorpe	(88)	1920	1928
Red Grange	(80)	1925	1934
Bronko Nagurski	(35)	1930	1943
Mel Hein	(74)	1931	1945
Don Hutson	(6)	1935	1945
Sammy Baugh	(11)	1937	1952
Sid Luckman	(39)	1939	1950
Steve Van Buren	(77)	1944	1951
Otto Graham	(7)	1946	1955
Marion Motley	(32)	1946	1955
Elroy Hirsch	(89)	1946	1957
Lou Groza	(99)	1946	1967
Emlen Tunnell	(70)	1948	1961
Bobby Layne	(52)	1948	1962
Chuck Bednarik	(54)	1949	1962
George Blanda	(98)	1949	1975
Jack Christiansen	(86)	1951	1958
Night Train Lane	(19)	1952	1965
Bill George	(49)	1952	1966
Gino Marchetti	(15)	1952	1966
Roosevelt Brown	(57)	1953	1965
Joe Schmidt	(65)	1953	1965
Raymond Berry	(40)	1955	1967
Lenny Moore	(71)	1956	1967
Sam Huff	(76)	1956	1969
Forrest Gregg	(28)	1956	1971
Bart Starr	(41)	1956	1971
Johnny Unitas	(5)	1956	1973
Jim Brown	(1)	1957	1965
Jim Parker	(24)	1957	1967
Willie Davis	(69)	1958	1969
Ray Nitschke	(18)	1958	1972
Larry Wilson	(43)	1960	1972
Jim Otto	(78)	1960	1974
Herb Adderley	(45)	1961	1972
Mike Ditka	(90)	1961	1972
Deacon Jones	(13)	1961	1974
Bob Lilly	(10)	1961	1974
Fran Tarkenton	(59)	1961	1978
Lance Alworth	(31)	1962	1972
Merlin Olsen	(25)	1962	1976
John Mackey	(48)	1963	1972
Bobby Bell	(66)	1963	1974
Buck Buchanan	(67)	1963	1975
Willie Brown	(50)	1963	1978
Charley Taylor	(85)	1964	1977
Paul Warfield	(60)	1964	1977
Gale Sayers	(21)	1965	1971
Dick Butkus	(9)	1965	1973
Joe Namath	(96)	1965	1977
Fred Biletnikoff	(94)	1965	1978
Lem Barney	(97)	1967	1977
Willie Lanier	(42)	1967	1977
Ken Houston	(61)	1967	1980
Larry Little	(79)	1967	1980
Alan Page	(34)	1967	1981
Gene Upshaw	(62)	1967	1981
Art Shell	(55)	1968	1982
O.J. Simpson	(26)	1969	1979
Roger Staubach	(29)	1969	1979
Joe Greene	(14)	1969	1981
Ted Hendricks	(64)	1969	1983
Charlie Joiner	(100)	1969	1986
Mel Blount	(36)	1970	1983
Terry Bradshaw	(44)	1970	1983
Jack Ham	(47)	1971	1982
Franco Harris	(83)	1972	1984
John Hannah	(20)	1973	1985
Dan Fouts	(92)	1973	1987
Jack Lambert	(30)	1974	1984
Mike Webster	(75)	1974	1990
Walter Payton	(8)	1975	1987
Randy White	(51)	1975	1988
Mike Haynes	(93)	1976	1989
Steve Largent	(46)	1976	1989
Tony Dorsett	(53)	1977	1988
Earl Campbell	(33)	1978	1985
Kellen Winslow	(73)	1979	1987
Joe Montana	(3)	1979	1994
Dwight Stephenson	(84)	1980	1987
Anthony Munoz	(17)	1980	1992
Art Monk	(91)	1980	1995
Mike Singletary	(56)	1981	1992
Lawrence Taylor	(4)	1981	1993
Ronnie Lott	(23)	1981	1994
Marcus Allen	(72)	1982	1997
Eric Dickerson	(38)	1983	1993
John Elway	(16)	1983	1998
Darrell Green	(81)	1983	1998
Dan Marino	(27)	1983	1998
Jerry Rice	(2)	1985	1998
Bruce Smith	(58)	1985	1998
Reggie White	(22)	1985	1998
Steve Young	(63)	1985	1998
Rod Woodson	(87)	1987	1998
Troy Aikman	(95)	1989	1998
Barry Sanders	(12)	1989	1998
Deion Sanders	(37)	1989	1998
Emmitt Smith	(68)	1990	1998
Brett Favre	(82)	1991	1998

Alphabetical Listing

Player	Rank	From	To
Adderley, Herb	(45)	1961	1972
Aikman, Troy	(95)	1989	1998
Allen, Marcus	(72)	1982	1997
Alworth, Lance	(31)	1962	1972
Barney, Lem	(97)	1967	1977
Baugh, Sammy	(11)	1937	1952
Bednarik, Chuck	(54)	1949	1962
Bell, Bobby	(66)	1963	1974
Berry, Raymond	(40)	1955	1967
Biletnikoff, Fred	(94)	1965	1978
Blanda, George	(98)	1949	1975
Blount, Mel	(36)	1970	1983
Bradshaw, Terry	(44)	1970	1983
Brown, Jim	(1)	1957	1965
Brown, Roosevelt	(57)	1953	1965
Brown, Willie	(50)	1963	1978
Buchanan, Buck	(67)	1963	1975
Butkus, Dick	(9)	1965	1973
Campbell, Earl	(33)	1978	1985
Christiansen, Jack	(86)	1951	1958
Davis, Willie	(69)	1958	1969
Dickerson, Eric	(38)	1983	1993
Ditka, Mike	(90)	1961	1972
Dorsett, Tony	(53)	1977	1988
Elway, John	(16)	1983	1998
Favre, Brett	(82)	1991	1998
Fouts, Dan	(92)	1973	1987
George, Bill	(49)	1952	1966
Graham, Otto	(7)	1946	1955
Grange, Red	(80)	1925	1934
Green, Darrell	(81)	1983	1998
Greene, Joe	(14)	1969	1981
Gregg, Forrest	(28)	1956	1971
Groza, Lou	(99)	1946	1967
Ham, Jack	(47)	1971	1982
Hannah, John	(20)	1973	1985
Harris, Franco	(83)	1972	1984
Haynes, Mike	(93)	1976	1989
Hein, Mel	(74)	1931	1945
Hendricks, Ted	(64)	1969	1983
Hirsch, Elroy	(89)	1946	1957
Houston, Ken	(61)	1967	1980
Huff, Sam	(76)	1956	1969
Hutson, Don	(6)	1935	1945
Joiner, Charlie	(100)	1969	1986
Jones, Deacon	(13)	1961	1974
Lambert, Jack	(30)	1974	1984
Lane, Night Train	(19)	1952	1965
Lanier, Willie	(42)	1967	1977
Largent, Steve	(46)	1976	1989
Layne, Bobby	(52)	1948	1962
Lilly, Bob	(10)	1961	1974
Little, Larry	(79)	1967	1980
Lott, Ronnie	(23)	1981	1994
Luckman, Sid	(39)	1939	1950
Mackey, John	(48)	1963	1972
Marchetti, Gino	(15)	1952	1966
Marino, Dan	(27)	1983	1998
Monk, Art	(91)	1980	1995
Montana, Joe	(3)	1979	1994
Moore, Lenny	(71)	1956	1967
Motley, Marion	(32)	1946	1955
Munoz, Anthony	(17)	1980	1992
Nagurski, Bronko	(35)	1930	1943
Namath, Joe	(96)	1965	1977
Nitschke, Ray	(18)	1958	1972
Olsen, Merlin	(25)	1962	1976
Otto, Jim	(78)	1960	1974
Page, Alan	(34)	1967	1981
Parker, Jim	(24)	1957	1967
Payton, Walter	(8)	1975	1987
Rice, Jerry	(2)	1985	1998
Sanders, Barry	(12)	1989	1998
Sanders, Deion	(37)	1989	1998
Sayers, Gale	(21)	1965	1971
Schmidt, Joe	(65)	1953	1965
Shell, Art	(55)	1968	1982
Simpson, O.J.	(26)	1969	1979
Singletary, Mike	(56)	1981	1992
Smith, Bruce	(58)	1985	1998
Smith, Emmitt	(68)	1990	1998
Starr, Bart	(41)	1956	1971
Staubach, Roger	(29)	1969	1979
Stephenson, Dwight	(84)	1980	1987
Tarkenton, Fran	(59)	1961	1978
Taylor, Charley	(85)	1964	1977
Taylor, Lawrence	(4)	1981	1993
Thorpe, Jim	(88)	1920	1928
Tunnell, Emlen	(70)	1948	1961
Unitas, Johnny	(5)	1956	1973
Upshaw, Gene	(62)	1967	1981
Van Buren, Steve	(77)	1944	1951
Warfield, Paul	(60)	1964	1977
Webster, Mike	(75)	1974	1990
White, Randy	(51)	1975	1988
White, Reggie	(22)	1985	1998
Wilson, Larry	(43)	1960	1972
Winslow, Kellen	(73)	1979	1987
Woodson, Rod	(87)	1987	1998
Young, Steve	(63)	1985	1998

26 O.J. SIMPSON

Like any good thoroughbred, O.J. Simpson was a creature of timing. He knew precisely when to dart, cut back and accelerate to the finish line—and he knew how to do it with style. The aura, the memory of a humpback, forward-leaning Simpson high-stepping his way through an opponent's secondary remain indelibly locked in the minds of everyone who saw him over a sometimes-agonizing, often-amazing 11-year NFL career.

Simpson was a charmer who could light up a stadium with a 90-yard dash or a room with his 100-watt personality. On the field, he was The Juice, Buffalo's swashbuckling 6-1, 212-pound lightning rod who might punish a tackler on one play, zip past him on the next. Off the field, he was outgoing, accommodating and easy to like with his million-dollar smile and Hollywood good looks. O.J.'s first brush with prominence came when he won the 1968 Heisman Trophy while playing for Southern California.

There would be even more glorious moments in the NFL, even though Simpson was restricted by generally weak Bills teams that qualified only one time for the playoffs. Operating as the team's only serious offensive weapon, O.J. won the first of four rushing titles in 1972 and powered his way into the history books a year later when he became the first 2,000-yard rusher in NFL history. Some consider his 1975 season, which produced 2,243 yards (1,817 rushing, 426 receiving) and 23 touchdowns, even better.

Many of those yards could be attributed to the Electric Company offensive line coach Lou Saban constructed for Simpson, but many were the result of the quickness, escape artistry and power he flashed

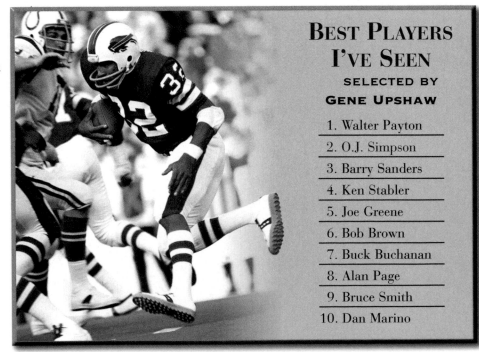

BEST PLAYERS I'VE SEEN

SELECTED BY GENE UPSHAW

1. Walter Payton
2. O.J. Simpson
3. Barry Sanders
4. Ken Stabler
5. Joe Greene
6. Bob Brown
7. Buck Buchanan
8. Alan Page
9. Bruce Smith
10. Dan Marino

with every graceful run. The six-time Pro Bowl selection retired in 1979, after two seasons in San Francisco, with 11,236 rushing yards and 2,142 more on 203 career receptions.

"JIM BROWN? I NEVER PLAYED AGAINST JIM BROWN.
BUT NOT IN MY WILDEST IMAGINATION DO I THINK JIM
BROWN COULD BE ANY BETTER THAN THE JUICE."

STEELERS DEFENSIVE END DWIGHT WHITE, 1976
THE SPORTING NEWS

"I'M PLAYING WITH A LEGEND.
DAN MARINO IS A LEGEND
IN HIS OWN TIME."

FORMER DOLPHINS RECEIVER
MARK CLAYTON, 1985
THE SPORTING NEWS

27

DAN MARINO

It all starts with what former Miami coach Don Shula called "the quickest arm I've ever seen." It also is strong, a deadly combination that has allowed Dan Marino to light up scoreboards for 16 seasons as the most prolific passer in NFL history. With one flick of his powerful right wrist, he can deliver a needle-threading rocket, drop a feathery floater between defenders or lay a 70-yard bomb on the fingertips of a full-stride sprinter. When it comes to throwing a football, nobody has ever done it better.

It's hard to argue against Marino as the best pure passer ever. His size (6-4, 228 pounds) gives him field vision and allows him to withstand constant punishment; his brash, almost cocky, personality gives him a competitive edge; his quick release allows him to wait longer for receivers and compensate for lack of mobility; and his arm strength enables him to make throws other quarterbacks can only dream about.

The poise and confidence have been there from the start, when Marino emerged from the University of Pittsburgh as the sixth quarterback selected in the 1983 draft. It has not been uncommon over the years to see him screaming at receivers and linemen about broken patterns and missed blocks. He's fiery, tough and desperate to win, characteristics that have earned him distinction as one of the game's most dangerous comeback quarterbacks.

The air show started in 1984 when Marino posted the most incredible passing season in history—5,084 yards, a .642 completion percentage and 48 touchdowns—and led the Dolphins to the only Super Bowl of his career, a loss to San Francisco. The absence of a championship on his resume has been a gnawing frustration for Marino, but it has been more reflective of the talent surrounding him. Still, the nine-time Pro Bowl selection entered 1999 as the career leader in every major passing category, including yards (58,913), completions (4,763) and touchdowns (408). His teams have reached the playoffs eight times, the AFC championship game on three occasions.

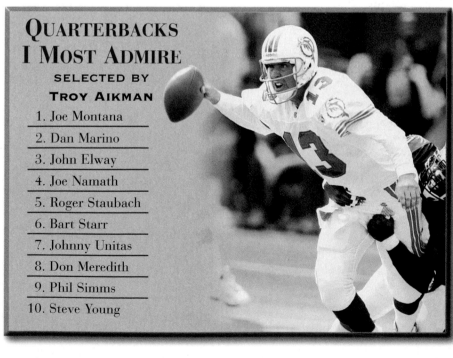

QUARTERBACKS I MOST ADMIRE

SELECTED BY TROY AIKMAN

1. Joe Montana
2. Dan Marino
3. John Elway
4. Joe Namath
5. Roger Staubach
6. Bart Starr
7. Johnny Unitas
8. Don Meredith
9. Phil Simms
10. Steve Young

"EXCELLENT TECHNIQUE AND
EXCELLENT FOOTWORK.
FORREST ALWAYS KEPT
HIMSELF PERFECTLY CENTERED.
HE AND ROSEY BROWN WERE
THE BEST TECHNICIANS OF ALL
THE OFFENSIVE LINEMEN.
AS A RUN-BLOCKER,
HE WAS OUTSTANDING."

LENNY MOORE,
1999

28

FORREST GREGG

Admirers called him the best dancer since Fred Astaire. Green Bay opponents called him masterful and frustrating. For Forrest Gregg, playing offensive tackle was all a matter of footwork and superior technique. Size was overrated. So was strength and power. Quickness was the name of his game and success was measured by his ability to do-si-do a bigger defensive end at the point of attack.

Nature dictated that finesse would play a major role in the life of the gruff, no-nonsense, straight-talking Gregg, who at 6-4 and 249 pounds was lighter and not as strong as the players he had to block. So he became a great technician. Gregg studied film on Jim Parker and Roosevelt Brown, two of the greatest linemen in football history. He worked hard on his footwork, learned about leverage and balance, studied film on opponents and mastered the sophisticated system of coach Vince Lombardi. He became the offensive anchor for one of the best teams ever assembled.

The feet would move up and down like well-oiled pistons as he maneuvered defenders away from the ball. Nobody beat the determined Gregg when he was protecting quarterback Bart Starr. He seldom made a mistake on run-blocking assignments, he was tireless and he was very intelligent, the ultimate team leader whom Lombardi called "the finest player I ever coached."

With the durable Gregg (he played in 187 consecutive games for the Packers over 14 seasons) clearing the way, the great Packers of the '60s won five NFL championships (and two Super Bowls) in a

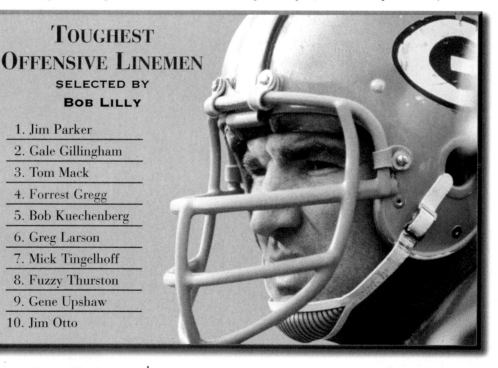

TOUGHEST OFFENSIVE LINEMEN
SELECTED BY
BOB LILLY

1. Jim Parker
2. Gale Gillingham
3. Tom Mack
4. Forrest Gregg
5. Bob Kuechenberg
6. Greg Larson
7. Mick Tingelhoff
8. Fuzzy Thurston
9. Gene Upshaw
10. Jim Otto

seven-year period. The nine-time Pro Bowl selection was lured out of retirement three times, twice to serve as a player/coach for the Packers and finally to finish his career with a Dallas Cowboys team that won a Super Bowl after the 1971 season.

"EVERY COWBOY, OFFENSE AND DEFENSE, LOOKED TO HIM. THEY ALL FELT THAT AS LONG AS HE WAS IN THE GAME, THEY HAD A CHANCE TO WIN. TO TELL YOU THE TRUTH, HIS OPPONENTS FELT THE SAME WAY."

FORMER CARDINALS COACH
JIM HANIFAN, 1980
THE SPORTING NEWS

29 ROGER STAUBACH

D on't be fooled by the clean-cut, All-American boy-next-door image. Roger Staubach, the always-polite U.S. Naval Academy graduate and Vietnam veteran, was a football warrior who could break your heart without remorse or regret. He could do it on the ground, through the air or in the huddle, a winning combination he supplied for 11 successful seasons as quarterback of the Dallas Cowboys.

Former coach Tom Landry called him "the greatest competitor I have ever seen," a quality that showed up over and over in Staubach's ability to engineer comeback victories. He did it 23 times in his career—14 in the final two minutes of a game. In a 1975 divisional playoff battle against the Minnesota Vikings, his desperation 50-yard bomb to Drew Pearson—the now-famous "Hail Mary pass"—gave the Cowboys a shocking 17-14 win.

That was the essence of Staubach, whose special mobility also set him apart from his peers. Game plans had to be carefully designed to contain Roger the Dodger, who was especially dangerous on third-down plays. He could scramble away from frustrated defenders and throw accurately on the run. His daring forays, the opposite of his soft-spoken, always-disciplined off-field personality, gave the Dallas offense an extra dimension.

Staubach's success is remarkable, considering he fulfilled a four-year commitment to the Navy and didn't become a professional until age 27. He played 11 years, threw for 22,700 yards and 153 touchdowns and ran for 2,264 yards. In his nine years as a starter, the Cowboys won 73 percent of their games, reached the playoffs eight times, won four NFC championship games and captured two of four Super Bowls. The four-time Pro Bowl selection, the 1963 Heisman Trophy winner at Navy, earned MVP honors in the Cowboys' Super Bowl VI victory over Miami.

BEST PLAYERS I'VE SEEN
SELECTED BY RAYMOND BERRY

1. Johnny Unitas	6. Otto Graham
2. Jim Brown	7. Bob Lilly
3. Lenny Moore	8. Roger Staubach
4. Gino Marchetti	9. Terry Bradshaw
5. Joe Montana	10. Barry Sanders

30 JACK LAMBERT

He was the toothless, snarling leader of Pittsburgh's Steel Curtain Defense. When Jack Lambert spoke, everybody listened—or else. He played the role of intimidating middle linebacker for 11 NFL seasons, six of them as the leading man for what many consider the greatest defensive unit ever assembled.

Jack the Ripper was taller (6-4) and lighter (220) than most middle linebackers of his era, but his Butkus-like intensity was front and center before every snap. The toothless snarl gave him an almost ghoulish look, as did the eyes that rolled madly inside a dark helmet. An excited voice would bark out defensive signals, arms would pump wildly and legs would quiver uncontrollably in anticipation of the punishment he was about to deliver.

And deliver he did, with vicious consistency. What Lambert lacked in weight, he more than made up for with speed and quickness to the ball. He was like a ballcarrier-seeking missile and his height presented problems for quarterbacks throwing over the middle. But what set Lambert apart from other middle linebackers was his ability to smother backs and tight ends in passing situations, a talent that produced 28 career interceptions.

Lambert might have played with a demonic fervor, but behind that facade was a soft-spoken, sensitive, intelligent leader who served as defensive captain from 1977 until his 1984 retirement. He spent most of his career surrounded by greatness—Joe Greene, L.C. Greenwood, Ernie Holmes up front, Jack Ham and Andy Russell on the outside, Mel Blount and Donnie

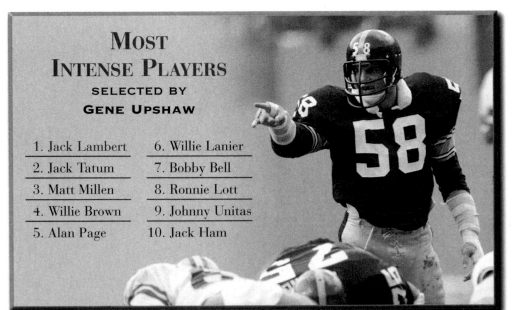

MOST INTENSE PLAYERS
SELECTED BY GENE UPSHAW

1. Jack Lambert	6. Willie Lanier
2. Jack Tatum	7. Bobby Bell
3. Matt Millen	8. Ronnie Lott
4. Willie Brown	9. Johnny Unitas
5. Alan Page	10. Jack Ham

Shell in the backfield—and he came to symbolize the work ethic required of a team playing in blue-collar Pittsburgh. It wasn't a coincidence that the Steelers won Super Bowls in four of Lambert's first six seasons and that he finished his career by playing in a then-record nine straight Pro Bowls.

"LAMBERT WAS EQUALLY GOOD AGAINST THE RUN AS THOSE OTHER GREAT LINEBACKERS, BUT HE WAS DRAMATICALLY BETTER THAN ANY OF THEM AGAINST THE PASS. HE CALLED THE DEFENSIVE SIGNALS. HE SET THE TONE. HE WAS INTELLIGENT, ALL BUSINESS, A TERRIFIC LEADER."

FORMER STEELERS LINEBACKER ANDY RUSSELL

"THE GOOD LORD USUALLY TAKES SOMETHING AWAY FROM AN INDIVIDUAL TO KEEP HIM FROM BEING PERFECT, BUT HE GOOFED WHEN HE CAME TO ALWORTH."

FORMER BRONCOS COACH
MAC SPEEDIE, 1968
THE SPORTING NEWS

31

LANCE ALWORTH

He was Bambi, the bounding, graceful wide receiver who eluded defensive backs like a startled deer might flee from a hunter. His long, loping stride, dance-stepping footwork and leaping, twisting style brought beauty to a sport filled with beasts. Lance Alworth was the ultimate wide receiver of the 1960s, a crowd-pleasing showpiece for the AFL in its battle to gain football respectability.

He joined the San Diego Chargers in 1962 and quickly blossomed into the AFL's first true superstar. It was a perfect match: Sid Gillman's high-powered vertical passing game with John Hadl throwing to the speedy Alworth, who was explosive, fearless and acrobatic. He never met a defender he couldn't burn, and he never saw a pass he couldn't catch, thanks to his outstanding leaping ability and what Gillman called "the greatest hands I've ever seen."

Throw in those big brown eyes, a Prince Valiant haircut, Hollywood good looks and the stylish clothes that became his trademark and you have star quality. Alworth made it all work over an 11-year career that produced 542 receptions for 10,266 yards and 85 touchdowns. He averaged a remarkable 18.9 yards per catch, recorded seven straight 1,000-yard seasons and caught at least one pass in every AFL game in which he played. His showcase season was 1965, when he caught 69 passes for 1,602 yards and 14 touchdowns—averaging a whopping 23.2 yards per reception.

Alworth, who helped the Chargers win the 1963 AFL championship, spent his final two years in Dallas,

TOUGHEST RECEIVERS TO COVER
SELECTED BY WILLIE BROWN

1. Lance Alworth
2. Charley Taylor
3. Jerry Rice
4. Paul Warfield
5. Charlie Joiner
6. Fred Biletnikoff
7. Charley Hennigan
8. Otis Taylor
9. Lionel Taylor
10. Ray Renfro

where his free-wheeling style was restricted by a more-conservative offense. Still, the seven-time Pro Bowl selection played a prominent role for the 1971 team that won a league championship, and he caught a TD pass in a Super Bowl VI win over Miami.

32  MARION MOTLEY

"HE HAD BIG, WIDE SHOULDERS AND HE WAS
A GREAT BLOCKER. HE WAS BIG AND STRONG
AND HAD GREAT SPEED FOR THE SIZE OF
MAN THAT HE WAS."

FORMER BROWNS RECEIVER
DANTE LAVELLI, 1999

is football destiny was charted at Canton, Ohio, in the 1930s and fulfilled many years later in the same city. Somewhere between his childhood and Hall of Fame election, Marion Motley discovered that superior athletic abilities could carry him to lasting fame as a social pioneer and a great fullback. But his ticket to greatness would not come without a price.

Motley, a hulking 6-1, 232-pound bulldozer, made his professional debut with the Cleveland Browns of the newly formed All-America Football Conference in 1946, joining teammate Bill Willis as the first blacks in the pro game since the early 1930s. Although they endured untold hardships and bigotry in the months preceding the 1947 baseball debut of Jackie Robinson, they never received equal credit for their social breakthroughs.

Motley made a different kind of impact on the field. A rookie at age 26, he became a one-man wrecking crew for the talented Paul Brown-constructed team that would dominate the AAFC and NFL over his eight pro seasons. Motley was a devastating force when he carried the ball on power sweeps or up the middle on his patented trap play. He was a take-no-prisoners blocker on running plays, a one-man wall for quarterback Otto Graham on passes and a capable receiver. He also was an outstanding linebacker and kickoff-return man in the AAFC.

BEST PLAYERS I'VE SEEN
SELECTED BY LENNY MOORE

1. Marion Motley	6. Joe Schmidt
2. Ollie Matson	7. Otto Graham
3. Jim Brown	8. Barry Sanders
4. Lawrence Taylor	9. Reggie White
5. Dick Butkus	10. Raymond Berry

When the Browns were accepted into the NFL in 1950, opponents got their first look at the new-era fullback—a blocker and runner with elusiveness instead of the traditional line plunger. They quickly designed defenses to stop him, but he still led the league in rushing. When Motley retired after the 1953 season (he made a brief 1955 comeback with Pittsburgh), he had compiled an amazing 5.7-yard rushing average in the AAFC/NFL and his teams had won five league championships and lost in the title game three times.

33

EARL CAMPBELL

You always could tell when the Earl Campbell Express was coming. The ground rumbled, bodies tumbled and fearless hearts crumbled. He was equal parts freight train, thoroughbred and warrior,

all blended into a heavily muscled, bowling ball-like 232-pound body. Campbell was raw power, a yard-eating machine that terrorized NFL defenders from 1978 through 1985.

To say that Campbell was not your everyday running back was something of an understatement. His 5-11 frame featured tree-trunk thighs that measured 36 inches, only two fewer than his waist, and a big, battering-ram head. He ran with a forward lean, providing a low center of gravity and a small margin of error for would-be tacklers. He was a sincere, no-nonsense East Texas Southern Baptist whose heart was as big as his massive thighs. He refused to give up on any run, taking great pride in dealing out punishment while gaining every possible inch.

Campbell exploded onto the NFL scene after a Heisman Trophy-winning senior season at the University of Texas. Playing for his home-state Houston Oilers, he rumbled for an NFL-leading 1,450 yards in his rookie season and followed that with league-leading seasons of 1,697 and 1,934. Through his first six seasons as the centerpiece of Houston's offense, Campbell averaged 1,383 yards rushing and helped the Oilers reach two AFC championship games.

BEST PLAYERS I'VE SEEN
SELECTED BY
STEVE LARGENT

1. Earl Campbell
2. Walter Payton
3. Jerry Rice
4. Dan Marino
5. Dan Fouts
6. John Elway
7. Kenny Easley
8. Ronnie Lott
9. Joe Greene
10. Randy White

The pride that prodded Campbell to stretch out every run over eight grueling seasons for the Oilers and New Orleans Saints also might have been responsible for his relatively short career. All the pounding he absorbed, all the bone-jarring blows from second, third and fourth tacklers wore down his body and prompted a premature drop-off in performance. When Campbell retired after the 1985 season, he had 9,407 yards (1,176 per season), 74 touchdowns and five Pro Bowl appearances.

"THE WAY CAMPBELL RUNS,
IT'S LIKE TRYING TO STOP
A TRUCK GOING DOWNHILL
WITHOUT A DRIVER. NOW
THAT'S HARD TO STOP."

FORMER BEARS COACH
NEILL ARMSTRONG, 1980
THE SPORTING NEWS

"WHEN I WAS WITH LOS ANGELES, I THOUGHT MERLIN OLSEN WAS THE BEST TACKLE AROUND. AND I'M SURE (DALLAS ASSISTANT) ERNIE STAUTNER FEELS BOB LILLY IS THE BEST. BUT RIGHT NOW, I THINK ALAN IS THE BEST TACKLE I HAVE EVER SEEN. HE DOES EVERYTHING YOU ASK, AND THEN SOME."

VIKINGS ASSISTANT COACH
JACK PATERA, 1970
THE SPORTING NEWS

34
ALAN PAGE

Call him the thinking man's defensive tackle, a destroyer who only employed contact as a means to an end. Alan Page never wore arm pads during his 15-year NFL career because he planned to go around blockers, not hit them. He relied on intelligence, speed and explosive quickness to win battles in the trenches, a style that allowed him to redefine the position over a Hall of

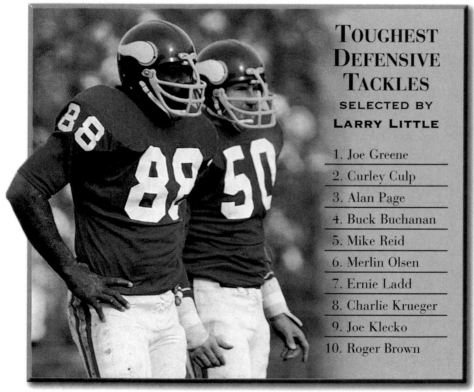

TOUGHEST DEFENSIVE TACKLES

SELECTED BY
LARRY LITTLE

1. Joe Greene
2. Curley Culp
3. Alan Page
4. Buck Buchanan
5. Mike Reid
6. Merlin Olsen
7. Ernie Ladd
8. Charlie Krueger
9. Joe Klecko
10. Roger Brown

brute force to blow past a blocker. Page's strengths were quickness off the snap and pursuit—a sideline-to-sideline determination to chase down the ball. His uncanny ability to get into the backfield gave him distinction as the game's first outstanding pass-rushing tackle and a dangerous kick-blocker.

A free-lancer within the Vikings' defensive system, Page became the centerpiece for the famed "Purple People Eaters" defense that carried Minnesota to Super Bowls after the 1969, 1973, 1974 and 1976 seasons—all losses. Page and end Jim Marshall formed a dynamic right side through most of the 1970s, with Carl Eller operating efficiently on the left. With the relentless, unemotional Page often controlling the flow of games from 1968 through 1977, the Vikings were 104-35-1.

Through all of his success, the nine-time Pro Bowl selection professed a take-it-or-leave-it feeling

Fame career that started with the Minnesota Vikings in 1967 and ended 218 games later in Chicago.

The 6-4, 245-pound Page was thinner than most tackles, but he also was quicker and faster. The former Notre Dame star played like a linebacker in a three-point stance, an aggressive attack man who didn't need

about football and earned a law degree before finishing his career. He also became fascinated with running and competed in marathons, a pastime that contributed to his late-career drop to 220 pounds and his 1978 breakup with the Vikings. He now is serving as an associate justice in the Minnesota Supreme Court.

35

BRONKO NAGURSKI

Bronko Nagurski was the stuff of which legends are made—a Paul Bunyanesque fullback who journeyed from a farm near Rainy River, Canada, to national acclaim as a two-position All-American at the University of Minnesota and to folk-hero status for the Chicago Bears. He was bigger than most linemen of his era, a rock-solid 6-2, 226-pounder with massive arms and hands, a size-19 neck and powerful shoulders that punished tacklers.

Nagurski bulled his way through the NFL with head down, legs churning and bodies flying. It often took four defenders to make a tackle: two to grab hold and slow him down, one to knock him off balance and one to finish him off. Nagurski also was a devastating defensive tackle/linebacker and one of the greatest 60-minute players. His career rushing totals, surprisingly low, could have been phenomenal if Bears coach George Halas had not valued him so highly on defense and as a blocker for the other thoroughbred backs he stockpiled on his roster.

Lost in the shadow of Nagurski's reputation as the ultimate power runner was his ability as a pioneer passer. It was Nagurski who made the championship-securing touchdown pass to Red Grange in a 1932 indoor playoff battle against Portsmouth. And he came back in the NFL's first official championship game a year later to throw for two TDs in a victory over New York. Nobody could dominate a game so thoroughly.

The man who came to symbolize the raw power and brute force of professional football played from 1930 to 1937, when he left the Bears in a salary dispute with Halas. He returned six years later to help the war-strapped Bears and contributed a touchdown run in their 1943 championship game win over Washington. Nagurski became a Hall of Fame charter member in 1963.

BEST PLAYERS I'VE SEEN
SELECTED BY LANCE ALWORTH

1. Barry Sanders
2. Walter Payton
3. John Elway
4. O.J. Simpson
5. Gale Sayers
6. Marcus Allen
7. Joe Namath
8. Bronko Nagurski
9. Dick Butkus
10. Reggie White

"THERE'S ONLY ONE WAY TO DEFENSE HIM—SHOOT HIM BEFORE HE LEAVES THE DRESSING ROOM. HE IS THE ONLY BACK I EVER SAW WHO RAN HIS OWN INTERFERENCE. SEE THESE LUMPS ON MY HEAD? I GOT MOST OF THEM TRYING TO STOP NAGURSKI."

FORMER GIANTS PLAYER STEVE OWEN

"I PLAYED IN A LOT OF PRO
BOWLS. I NEVER SAW
A CORNERBACK LIKE HIM.
HE WAS THE MOST INCREDIBLE
ATHLETE I HAVE EVER SEEN.
WITH MEL, YOU COULD TAKE
ONE WIDE RECEIVER
AND JUST WRITE HIM OFF.
HE COULD HANDLE ANYBODY
IN THE LEAGUE."

JACK HAM

36
MEL BLOUNT

L ove him, hate him. The choice was simple for Pittsburgh fans, who enjoyed 14 glorious seasons with one of the great cornerbacks in NFL history. For everybody else, the tall, almost sinister figure of

Mel Blount—the Darth Vaderish man in black—symbolized the evil intentions of a Steel Curtain defense that shrouded the league through much of the 1970s.

Blount was the best athlete on the Steelers' talent-filled roster, maybe even in the league. He had great size (6-3, 205) for a corner, but he matched his contemporaries in quickness and speed and he had the power and toughness of a linebacker. Blount was the prototype cornerback of his era, maybe the best bump-and-run pass defender ever. He ran with the speedy wideouts stride for stride and his aggressive pounding of receivers only added to his intimidating persona.

Blount, a tireless worker who refined his skills while frustrating Steelers stars Lynn Swann and John Stallworth in practice, was cocky enough to believe that nobody could beat him one-on-one. He also was a punishing run-support tackler and a durable performer who missed only one

regular-season game because of injury. The physical style perfected by the Steelers' secondary prompted NFL officials to outlaw the bump-and-run, but Blount adjusted and continued to thrive.

Quarterbacks had to be wary of the former Southern University star, who, apparently beaten, would swoop out of nowhere to knock away or pick off

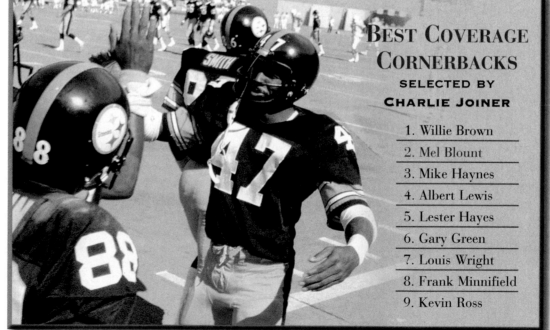

BEST COVERAGE CORNERBACKS
SELECTED BY CHARLIE JOINER

1. Willie Brown
2. Mel Blount
3. Mike Haynes
4. Albert Lewis
5. Lester Hayes
6. Gary Green
7. Louis Wright
8. Frank Minnifield
9. Kevin Ross

passes with his long arms. A five-time Pro Bowl player, he made 57 career interceptions, including a league-leading 11 in 1975. But his greatest legacy was membership on a Steelers team that played in six AFC championship games and won four Super Bowls.

37

DEION SANDERS

Look for the sparkling jewelry, the engaging smile and the confident, almost arrogant strut. Those are dead giveaways that Deion Sanders is preening for the cameras and media hordes he consistently attracts.

Prime Time is always working the angles, whether perpetuating his glitzy off-field image or enhancing his reputation as the best—and most stylish—coverage cornerback in the NFL—a reputation borne of superior athleticism and in-your-face, never-give-an-inch confidence.

Sanders is foremost a playmaker who uses blazing speed to energize his team and sting opposing clubs in every way imaginable. He can score on an interception, electrify a crowd with a dazzling punt return, go deep as an occasional wide receiver or take a handoff on an end-around. Sanders produced five plays of 55 yards or longer for the Dallas Cowboys in 1998—one interception return, three punt returns, one reception—and scored three touchdowns, giving him 20 for his career.

It's all in the magnificent legs that get him around the field faster than anybody else. Sanders is not technically superior, but he uses his speed to erase mistakes and catch up with apparently open receivers. He's especially dangerous when covering square-outs, where he accelerates aggressively to the ball. Wary coordinators have been known to concede an entire side of the field

to the seven-time Pro Bowl selection.

The athleticism vaulted Sanders into prominence in 1989 when he played his first NFL season with Atlanta and doubled as a basestealing center fielder for the New York Yankees—a two-sport act in the mold of Bo Jackson. Deion continued his off-and-on baseball

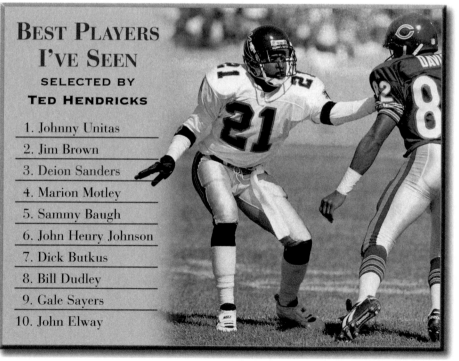

BEST PLAYERS I'VE SEEN
SELECTED BY TED HENDRICKS

1. Johnny Unitas
2. Jim Brown
3. Deion Sanders
4. Marion Motley
5. Sammy Baugh
6. John Henry Johnson
7. Dick Butkus
8. Bill Dudley
9. Gale Sayers
10. John Elway

career through 1997 and even played in a World Series with the Atlanta Braves. But his greatest success has come as a smothering corner and dangerous return man, helping San Francisco win a Super Bowl after the 1994 season and the Cowboys do the same the following year.

"I CAN'T REMEMBER SEEING ANY BACK WITH MORE TALENT AND
POTENTIAL THAN ERIC, AND THAT INCLUDES MYSELF AND GALE SAYERS.
HE IS THE BEST I'VE SEEN, AND I MEAN EVER."

O.J. SIMPSON, 1984

38

ERIC DICKERSON

You couldn't help but notice the glide, the way his feet seemed to hydroplane over a football surface like a speedboat barely touching water. Or the remarkable acceleration that shot Eric Dickerson through the slightest crack in an opponent's line. He was instant offense, a touchdown waiting to happen. And he was one of the game's spectacular running backs over a sometimes-phenomenal 11-year NFL career.

The tall, muscular, good-looking former SMU star was easy to spot. Off the field, he was charismatic, the man you would notice in a crowded room. On the field, he looked like something out of Star Wars—clear goggles, a facemask with four horizontal bars, a protective neck collar, extra reinforced shoulder pads, a flak jacket, elbow pads and tape covering his shoes. The colorful yellow-and-blue Los Angeles Rams uniform and his explosive, upright running style were like exclamation points.

Dickerson became an NFL prodigy in 1983 when he posted record rookie numbers of 390 carries, 1,808 yards, 51 receptions and 20 touchdowns for the suddenly respectable Rams. It was the first of seven straight 1,000-yard seasons and a fitting appetizer for the spectacular 1984 performance that netted a season rushing record of 2,105 yards. Opponents marveled at his long-striding burst, which allowed Dickerson to run around tacklers and avoid the Jim Brown-like punishment he openly disdained.

Dickerson's Rams career was cut short after three 1987 games by a contract dispute. A spectacular three-team, 10-player trade landed him in Indianapolis, where he continued to churn out big yardage for the lowly Colts. Dickerson, who ended his career with one-

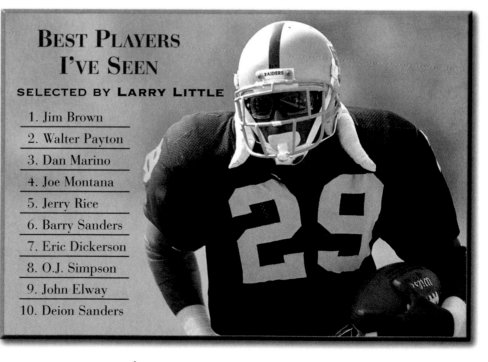

BEST PLAYERS I'VE SEEN

SELECTED BY LARRY LITTLE

1. Jim Brown
2. Walter Payton
3. Dan Marino
4. Joe Montana
5. Jerry Rice
6. Barry Sanders
7. Eric Dickerson
8. O.J. Simpson
9. John Elway
10. Deion Sanders

year stops in Los Angeles (the Raiders) and Atlanta, never played on a championship team, but his impressive ledger included 13,259 rushing yards (third all-time), 2,137 receiving yards on 281 catches and six Pro Bowl appearances.

39

SID LUCKMAN

"I'VE NEVER SEEN A PLAYER WHO WORKED AS HARD AS LUCKMAN. WHEN EVERYONE ELSE LEFT THE PRACTICE FIELD, HE STAYED ON. HE PRACTICED PIVOTING AND BALL-HANDLING BY THE HOUR. WHEN HE WENT TO HIS ROOM AT NIGHT, HE STOOD BEFORE A MIRROR AND PRACTICED STILL MORE. HE BECAME A GREAT PLAYER SIMPLY BECAUSE HE DEVOTED ABOUT 400 PERCENT MORE EFFORT TO IT THAN MOST ATHLETES ARE WILLING TO DO."

GEORGE HALAS, 1947

The first things you noticed about Sid Luckman were his easy smile, square chin, high forehead and dark, rugged good lucks. But the smile disappeared when the former Brooklyn street kid pulled a Chicago Bears helmet over his thick, curly black hair and went to work as chief executor of a George Halas winning machine that produced four NFL championships in the 1940s.

Luckman, a former single-wing star at Columbia University, brought the perfect blend of physical and leadership abilities to his 12-season role as pro football's first successful T-formation quarterback. He was equal parts magician and field general, a gifted ball-handler who could misdirect the defense and set up Chicago runners for big gains or receivers for his deadly deep passes.

Luckman will forever be linked with contemporary Sammy Baugh as the passing quarterbacks who changed the offensive course of pro football, but Luckman was the first to do it from the formation that would become the rage of the NFL. He threw over the top with picture-perfect form and was known for his deep-striking ability while the always-scrambling, off-balance Baugh preferred the controlled possession passing attack.

Luckman, who also was a capable punter and kick returner, was so valuable to the Bears that Halas restricted his running, hoping to avoid injury. So he overpowered opponents in other ways, never in more devastating fashion than the 1940 championship game. With fans and NFL officials watching in amazement, Luckman directed the Bears past Baugh's Washington Redskins, 73-0, dramatically demonstrating the explosive possibilities of the T-formation. He finished his career in 1950 with 14,686 passing yards and threw a record seven of his 137 career touchdown passes in a 1943 game and five more in the 1943 championship game win over Washington.

BEST QUARTERBACKS I'VE SEEN
SELECTED BY SAMMY BAUGH

Sid Luckman
Johnny Unitas
John Elway
Dan Marino
Otto Graham
Joe Namath
Sonny Jurgensen
Bobby Layne
Davey O'Brien
Joe Montana

40 RAYMOND BERRY

He looked out of place in a football locker room—a kitten in a room full of big, snarling dogs. The gangly build, the glasses and the shy, professorial look sentenced Raymond Berry to life as a football enigma. But what you saw was not what you got from Berry, who teamed for 12 of his 13 seasons with Baltimore quarterback Johnny Unitas as one of the most prolific passing combinations in NFL history.

The shy, reticent Berry was not blessed with NFL-like athleticism. He wore a corset for his bad back, he was nearsighted and he had above-average, but not spectacular, speed. What he did have was determination, a work ethic and creativity that constantly amazed coaches and teammates. His practices started early and ended well after the locker room had cleared. He studied film at home, caught backyard passes from his wife and invented sun goggles, wrist bands and other gimmicks that quickly became a part of the Berry mystique.

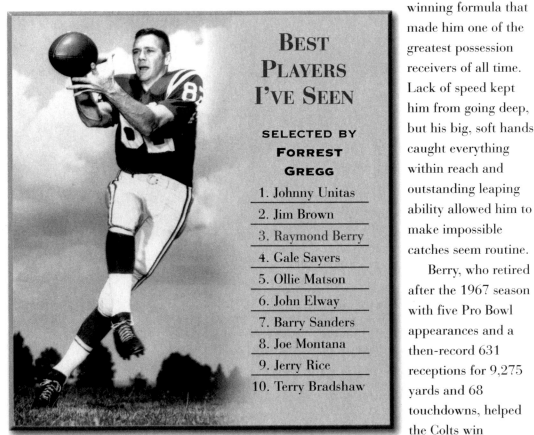

BEST PLAYERS I'VE SEEN

SELECTED BY FORREST GREGG

1. Johnny Unitas
2. Jim Brown
3. Raymond Berry
4. Gale Sayers
5. Ollie Matson
6. John Elway
7. Barry Sanders
8. Joe Montana
9. Jerry Rice
10. Terry Bradshaw

Attention to detail is what gave Berry his edge—and it showed with every move, every precise pass route that confounded NFL defensive backs. He figured out ways to beat them and then executed a winning formula that made him one of the greatest possession receivers of all time. Lack of speed kept him from going deep, but his big, soft hands caught everything within reach and outstanding leaping ability allowed him to make impossible catches seem routine.

Berry, who retired after the 1967 season with five Pro Bowl appearances and a then-record 631 receptions for 9,275 yards and 68 touchdowns, helped the Colts win consecutive NFL championships in 1958 and 1959. His defining moment came in the classic 1958 title game against the New York Giants when he caught 12 passes for 178 yards and a touchdown.

"ME AND GINO (MARCHETTI) WOULD HAVE
A DOZEN BEERS DOWN AFTER PRACTICE
AND RAYMOND WOULD STILL BE OUT ON
THE FIELD CATCHING PASSES. WE'D ALL
BE RUNNING OFF THE PRACTICE FIELD AND
HE'D BE CHASING US TO GET SOMEBODY
TO THROW HIM ANOTHER 50 PASSES.
HE WAS ONE OF A KIND."

ART DONOVAN
FORMER COLTS TACKLE

41

BART STARR

Contrary to popular belief, perfection did not come easily for Bart Starr. He was an unlikely success story, a legend spawned largely on the sideline at the University of Alabama, in the 17th round of the NFL draft and from deep on the depth chart of a struggling franchise. Starr ran a quarterback sneak on professional football, rising to Hall of Fame prominence as the perfect field general for the near-perfect team of the 1960s.

On the surface, Starr's long and prosperous association with Vince Lombardi's colorful, blue-collar Green Bay Packers seemed strange. He was a Southern-bred boy, an always-polite "yes sir, no sir" kind of guy with deep religious convictions and no vices. But when Lombardi took the Packers' reins in 1959, the qualities he saw in Starr were a perfect match for his ball-control vision: quiet, calculating and always under control, both physically and emotionally.

Handed control of the meticulous, grinding, Green Bay offense, Starr led the Packers on a nine-year winning odyssey (1959-67) that produced an 89-29-4 record, six title-game appearances and five championships, including wins (and Starr MVPs) in the first two Super Bowls. Starr took Lombardi's well-conceived game plans and executed them with cool efficiency, deviating from script only with perfect audibles. Norm Van Brocklin, after watching Starr carve up his Minnesota Vikings in one game, called him "the smartest

quarterback in pro football."

Unlike swashbuckling, gambling contemporary Johnny Unitas, Starr was conservative and always threw the high-percentage pass. His accuracy was uncanny (a 57.4 percent career completion rate), and he once threw 294 passes without an interception. Starr, who finished his 16-year career in 1971 with

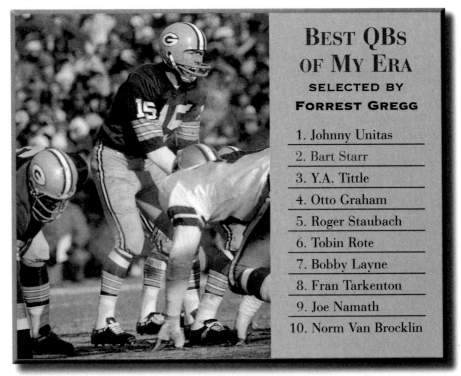

BEST QBs OF MY ERA
SELECTED BY FORREST GREGG

1. Johnny Unitas
2. Bart Starr
3. Y.A. Tittle
4. Otto Graham
5. Roger Staubach
6. Tobin Rote
7. Bobby Layne
8. Fran Tarkenton
9. Joe Namath
10. Norm Van Brocklin

24,718 passing yards, always will be remembered for his NFL championship-securing, 1-yard touchdown dive in the waning seconds of the Packers' 1967 "Ice Bowl" victory over Dallas.

42

WILLIE LANIER

Willie Lanier leans his 6-1, 245-pound body forward, ready to pounce with cat-like quickness. His steely glare locks into the concerned eyes of a quarterback who seems mesmerized by the

34-inch waist, 50-inch chest and 20-inch neck that soon will come crashing toward him like a heat-seeking missile. The fear is overpowering, but nothing compared with the havoc that will unfold once the ball is snapped.

Such was the aura of Lanier, the powerful "Honey Bear" who patrolled the middle of Kansas City's defense as a run-stuffing force from 1967 to '77. He was the premier defensive quarterback of the AFL and he gained Dick Butkus and Ray Nitschke-like star status after the AFL-NFL merger.

The smiling, easy-to-like Lanier transformed himself into a fierce, never-give-an-inch, ballhawking demon when he pulled on his red-and-white No. 63 Chiefs jersey. He was immovable on runs up the middle and obsessive when tracking down ballcarriers, who usually remembered the intense blows he delivered. Lanier, who had been a small-college All-American from Morgan State, also was fast enough to make 27 career interceptions while covering tight ends and running backs.

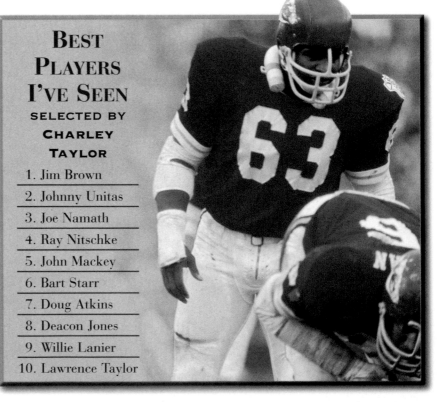

BEST PLAYERS I'VE SEEN
SELECTED BY **CHARLEY TAYLOR**

1. Jim Brown
2. Johnny Unitas
3. Joe Namath
4. Ray Nitschke
5. John Mackey
6. Bart Starr
7. Doug Atkins
8. Deacon Jones
9. Willie Lanier
10. Lawrence Taylor

With the quick-thinking Lanier centering an elite linebacking corps that included Bobby Bell and Jim Lynch, the Chiefs battled the Oakland Raiders for AFL dominance in the late

1960s and advanced to Super Bowl IV in 1970, when they defeated Minnesota. Lanier's road to the Hall of Fame was paved with All-Pro, All-AFL and All-NFL citations and he was named to the first six AFC-NFC Pro Bowl games, winning defensive MVP honors in 1971.

"IT (A WILLIE LANIER TACKLE)
REALLY WASN'T MUCH.
PART OF ME LANDED ONE PLACE
AND THE REST OF ME
SOMEPLACE ELSE. I PULLED
MYSELF TOGETHER AND WENT ON
JUST LIKE A MOUNTAIN
HAD NEVER FALLEN ON ME."

FORMER RAIDERS RUNNING BACK
HEWRITT DIXON

43

LARRY WILSON

He was the bane of every quarterback's existence, the player most likely to deliver physical and mental pain. His 6-0, 190-pound body was a cleverly disguised wrecking machine. Whether dashing madly into an opposing backfield—he was the pioneer of the safety blitz—or aggressively defending against the pass, Larry Wilson spent 13 seasons spreading his special kind of fear around the NFL.

It was a fear born out of respect for the oft-described "toughest player in the game." Wilson was a football bulldog, a free safety for the St. Louis Cardinals who played through incredible pain and never conceded a down. Former New York Giants coach Allie Sherman called Wilson "the goingest player I ever saw." Others called him the NFL player who coaxed more out of his abilities than any other.

Wilson's reckless style inspired Cardinals defensive coordinator Chuck Drulis' innovative idea for the safety blitz—code name "Wildcat." From 1960 to 1972, the former University of Utah halfback shot the gaps of offensive lines, making life miserable for quarterbacks and setting himself up for nasty blows from much-bigger blocking backs. When Wilson stayed back in coverage, he was a different kind of Wildcat—a great open-field tackler and an instinctive pass defender with an uncanny knack for getting to the ball.

Over his Hall of Fame career, Wilson, an eight-time Pro Bowl selection, intercepted 52 passes, including a league-leading 10 in 1966. But it was one he made in 1965 that brought him everlasting fame. Playing with casts on both of his broken hands, he leaped high to block a pass by Steelers quarterback Bill Nelsen, cradled the deflection in his arms and ran the ball back 35 yards, setting up a touchdown. The play was vintage Larry Wilson.

BEST PLAYERS I'VE SEEN
SELECTED BY JIM PARKER

1. John Brodie	6. Merlin Olsen
2. Jim Brown	7. Forrest Gregg
3. Jerry Rice	8. Jim Taylor
4. Night Train Lane	9. Reggie White
5. Larry Wilson	10. Paul Hornung

"You've got to hand it to Bradshaw;
he's bursting with talent.
My God, his arm is like a rifle."

Former Steelers quarterback
Terry Hanratty, 1972
The Sporting News

44

TERRY BRADSHAW

They called him buffoon, rube and country bumpkin. They cracked jokes about his rural naivete and suggested he was dumb. But Terry Bradshaw, he of the sparkling blue eyes, sly smile and dimpled chin,

had everyone fooled. He was dumb like a fox. And naive enough to lead the Pittsburgh Steelers to four Super Bowl championships over a fascinating 14-year career.

It all seemed so simple in 1970 when the lowly Steelers grabbed Bradshaw out of tiny Louisiana Tech with the No. 1 overall pick. Everyone predicted the 6-3, 215-pound phenom with the rifle arm, quick release and running back speed would lead the franchise to long-awaited respectability. But Bradshaw was a diamond in the rough, a small-town boy unprepared for the sophisticated professional game. His first few seasons were a struggle, both on the field and off.

And then, like magic, he blossomed into a big-play machine. Bradshaw's incredible deep touch began producing long touchdown passes to Lynn Swann and John Stallworth. His short passing game and scrambling ability confused defenses. His play-calling became clever and efficient. And his reputation grew as one of the great postseason performers in football history. When Bradshaw earned consecutive MVPs with a combined 627 passing yards and six touchdowns in Super Bowl XIII and XIV, he wiped

away the early-career putdowns and frustrations.

Throughout his career, Bradshaw was exciting and unpredictable. He could throw an 80-yard touchdown pass on one play, an interception into triple coverage on the next. He also was unpredictable in his

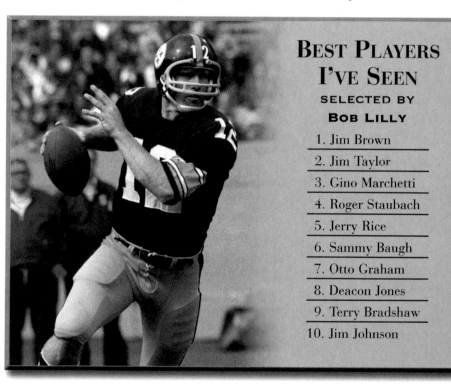

BEST PLAYERS I'VE SEEN
SELECTED BY
BOB LILLY

1. Jim Brown
2. Jim Taylor
3. Gino Marchetti
4. Roger Staubach
5. Jerry Rice
6. Sammy Baugh
7. Otto Graham
8. Deacon Jones
9. Terry Bradshaw
10. Jim Johnson

personal life, a free-spirited, fun-loving celebrity who dabbled in everything from business to country singing and acting. When he retired in 1983 with 27,989 passing yards and 212 TD passes, longtime Steelers owner Art Rooney called him the greatest quarterback of all time.

45

HERB ADDERLEY

The longest route to the Green Bay end zone was through the left side of the defense. If big end Willie Davis didn't get you, cornerback Herb Adderley would. When offensive coordinators designed game plans

against Vince Lombardi's Packers, it was pretty obvious where most of the plays would be headed. And it was a pretty good bet the team's top receiver would not be much of a factor.

The 6-0, 205-pound Adderley had only himself to blame for his sometimes-diminished role. He was the consummate one-on-one coverage back, the guy who could take a big-play receiver out of the offense. Teams that tried to run around Adderley's end also were frustrated by the aggressive, physical tackler who seldom missed his target.

Adderley's style was not immediately embraced by his two professional coaches—Lombardi from 1961 to '69 and Dallas' Tom Landry from 1970 to '72. He liked to play off the receiver and use his speed to attack the ball.

BEST CORNERS I'VE FACED
SELECTED BY PAUL WARFIELD

1. Mel Blount	6. Erich Barnes
2. Willie Brown	7. Irv Cross
3. Lem Barney	8. Bob Jeter
4. Herb Adderley	9. Brady Keys
5. Emmitt Thomas	10. Pat Fischer

He was quick, instinctive and smart, a gambler who could go for the big play. The speedy Adderley seldom dropped a ball and was dangerous and creative on returns—both on interceptions and kickoffs.

Seldom did he make a mistake, which only added to the luster of his 48 career interceptions and 21.8-yard return average on pickoffs. It's no coincidence that the confident, easy-to-like Adderley was a starter for two of the premier defenses of his era. First he helped the Packers win five championships (and two Super Bowls) in a seven-year span. Then he helped the Cowboys reach two Super Bowls and claim one title in three years. A five-time Pro Bowl choice who played in four of the first six Super Bowls, Adderley missed only three games in his first 11 seasons.

"I'M JUST THANKFUL HE'S PLAYING FOR THE PACKERS.
HE'S THE BEST CORNERBACK I'VE EVER SEEN."

BART STARR

"WHEN I GOT HERE AND HAD A CHANCE
TO WATCH HIM ON A REGULAR BASIS,
I WAS AMAZED. IN MY MIND, YOU CAN
TAKE EVERY SUPERLATIVE YOU CAN THINK
OF AND APPLY IT TO STEVE LARGENT.
HE'S THAT GOOD."

FORMER SEAHAWKS G.M.
MIKE MCCORMACK, 1984
THE SPORTING NEWS

46

STEVE LARGENT

Call him the master of illusion. When Steve Largent ran pass patterns, he always ended up here and the defender over there. That was the special magic of the record-setting wide receiver, who emptied his bag of tricks over a 14-year career with the Seattle Seahawks. When Largent zigged, everyone else in the stadium usually zagged.

Longtime Raiders cornerback Lester Hayes called him "the master of tomfoolery," a reference to Largent's ability to deceive cornerbacks. But he also will be remembered as a consummate pro who squeezed everything from his ability with a meticulous, cerebral approach to his craft. He didn't have great speed and had less than ideal size (5-11, 187), but he more than made up for those shortcomings with exceptional lateral quickness, great balance, body control and soft hands that seemed to pull balls in like a magnet.

Covering Largent was like a game of cat and mouse. He could run the same pattern on three straight plays and beat the cornerback in three different ways. He would use a move

on one play to set up a later one, throw two or three incomprehensible moves into one feint and run unusual routes that played with the defender's mind. Largent was unsurpassed in his preparation, a picture of total concentration. It was all part of a precise plan, conceived and executed by pro football's ultimate possession receiver.

Largent was a 1976 fourth-round pick of the Houston Oilers but was traded during his first training camp to the Seahawks for a 1977 eighth-round pick. By 1989, he had carved out his place as the greatest pass catcher in NFL history. When he retired, he owned records for most catches (819), yards (13,089) and touchdowns (100), all marks that have since been broken, and his eight 1,000-yard seasons still rank second only to Jerry Rice's 12. Largent, who once caught passes in 177 consecutive games, earned seven Pro Bowl selections.

BEST RECEIVERS I'VE SEEN
SELECTED BY CHARLIE JOINER

1. Jerry Rice	6. John Jefferson
2. Paul Warfield	7. Wes Chandler
3. Otis Taylor	8. Andre Reed
4. Steve Largent	9. James Lofton
5. Fred Biletnikoff	10. Cris Carter

47

JACK HAM

He was affectionately called "Dobre Shunka" (Great Ham) by Pittsburgh's Slovak fans. He was respectfully called Master Jack by opponents he faced on Sunday afternoons. Jack Ham was the brains behind the Steel Curtain brawn, the steadying hand for one of football's great defenses. When trouble loomed, he always was there with the big play.

As the outside linebacker on the left side of a defense fronted by Joe Greene and L.C. Greenwood, the 6-1, 225-pound former Penn State star didn't have to play the power game. He had explosive quickness and the savvy to diagnose plays, frustrating offensive coordinators who marveled at his anticipation and ability to carve up their game plans. The athletic Ham didn't mind delivering a blow, but he preferred to operate with intelligence and a consistent, unemotional discipline.

Surrounded by Greene, Greenwood, cornerback Mel Blount and fellow linebackers Jack Lambert and Andy Russell, Ham could be used like an extra defensive back, a role he relished. He loved the challenge of covering fleet running backs and tight ends and his ballhawking ability produced 32 interceptions over a 12-year career that started in 1971. He also recovered 19 opponent fumbles and was a dangerous kick-blocker.

Ironically, the low-key, quiet Ham, who went out of his way to avoid the spotlight, became one of the most popular players in a city that revered its blue-collar heroes. Ham wasn't as imposing as Lambert and he didn't hit as hard as Greene, but his guile-over-power style still caught the fancy of fans in the Steel City. The eight-time Pro Bowl selection played in six AFC title games in eight years and led the Steelers to four Super Bowl championships in six seasons before retiring after injury-plagued 1981 and 1982 seasons.

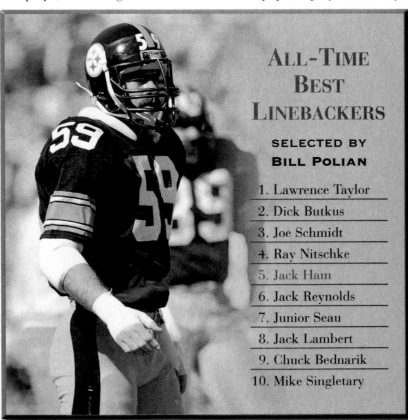

ALL-TIME BEST LINEBACKERS

SELECTED BY BILL POLIAN

1. Lawrence Taylor
2. Dick Butkus
3. Joe Schmidt
4. Ray Nitschke
5. Jack Ham
6. Jack Reynolds
7. Junior Seau
8. Jack Lambert
9. Chuck Bednarik
10. Mike Singletary

"He is the premier outside linebacker in football. He's the guy you measure other outside linebackers against."

Former Rams defensive tackle
Merlin Olsen, 1977
The Sporting News

"ONCE HE CATCHES THE BALL,
THE GREAT ADVENTURE
BEGINS. THOSE PEOPLE ON
DEFENSE CLIMB ALL OVER HIM.
THE LUCKY ONES FALL OFF.
OTHERS MIGHT BE TRAMPLED."

FORMER COLTS
ASSISTANT COACH
DICK BIELSKI, 1969
THE SPORTING NEWS

48
JOHN MACKEY

Nothing could prepare a wide-eyed defensive back for the sight of 224-pound John Mackey, ball tucked safely under a massive arm, rumbling straight at him full-speed. He was like a runaway truck,

a bulldozer on a mission. Mackey was willing to run around, over or through would-be tacklers, and those who successfully brought him down absorbed serious punishment while doing so.

Mackey was a fullback in tight end's clothing. He was a dangerous weapon in the passing arsenal of Johnny Unitas when most teams used their tight ends primarily as blockers. Mackey had the power to catch short slants, outs and screens and then use his powerful legs to churn out extra yardage. But he also had the speed to go deep, a tight end quality coaches had never had to defend against before. He was simply too elusive for the linebackers assigned to cover him and too big for the smaller defensive backs caught in one-on-one situations.

Fullback or tight end? That was the question Baltimore Colts coach Don Shula had to answer in 1963 when Mackey was drafted out of Syracuse, and his decision revolutionized the position. The soft-spoken, mild-mannered Mackey was a willing prototype—a devastating blocker against defensive ends and linebackers, a reliable pass catcher and a running force on end-around plays.

Mackey's big-play ability was demonstrated in 1966, when six of his nine touchdowns were scored on

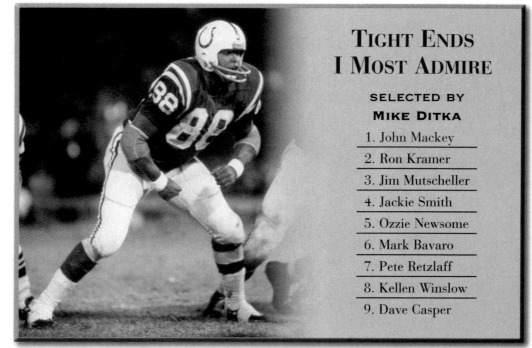

TIGHT ENDS I MOST ADMIRE

SELECTED BY MIKE DITKA

1. John Mackey
2. Ron Kramer
3. Jim Mutscheller
4. Jackie Smith
5. Ozzie Newsome
6. Mark Bavaro
7. Pete Retzlaff
8. Kellen Winslow
9. Dave Casper

plays of more than 50 yards. Twice he compiled season averages of more than 20 yards per catch and his 10-year career average of 15.8 was remarkable for a tight end. A five-time Pro Bowl choice and member of two Super Bowl teams (one winner), Mackey was voted the tight end on the NFL's 50th anniversary team in 1969.

"A PLAYER MUST HAVE AN INSTINCT FOR LINEBACKING
TO BE GOOD AT IT. BILL GEORGE HAS IT. HE DOESN'T
COMMIT HIMSELF TOO QUICKLY. HE'S MOTIONLESS UNTIL
HE SENSES WHERE A PLAY IS GOING, THEN—WHAM!—
HE MOVES LIKE LIGHTNING TO THE RIGHT PLACE."

FORMER BEARS COACH GEORGE HALAS

49

BILL GEORGE

H e didn't hit with Chuck Bednarik savagery or dominate with Dick Butkus intensity, but nobody can deny Bill George his distinction as one of the great middle linebackers in football history. He was the

first to play the position and the man who defined the way it would be played for generations to come. His innovative standup routine changed the course of defensive football.

George was a 6-2, 237-pound middle guard operating in the Chicago Bears' basic 5-2 defense when he first stood up, took a step back and began operating as a third linebacker. He had the quickness and speed to rush the passer, chase down a ballcarrier or defend against short passes in the new 4-3 scheme. But more exciting to coach George Halas was the way George grasped the Bears' complicated defensive schemes— and his ability to smell out plays before they happened.

Through most of a 15-year career that started in 1952, George served as Halas' defensive captain and signal-caller. A Wake Forest product with the closely cropped black hair and thick eyebrows, George diligently studied film, filled notebooks with opponent tendencies and prepared meticulously for each game. Not only was he totally prepared to perform his job, he understood the nuances of every position in every possible situation. His intelligence and uncanny ability to call for the perfect defensive formation just before every snap unnerved many quarterbacks.

George, who had explosive quickness off the snap, also was a dangerous inside blitzer and a pass defender who made 18 career interceptions. Thanks in large part to a defense designed around George, the 1963 Bears rolled to an 11-1-2 record, the Western

BEST LINEBACKERS I'VE SEEN
SELECTED BY MIKE DITKA

1. Dick Butkus	6. Jack Ham
2. Ray Nitschke	7. Jack Lambert
3. Mike Singletary	8. Chuck Howley
4. Joe Schmidt	9. Willie Lanier
5. Bill George	10. Sam Huff

Conference title and an NFL championship. The eight-time Pro Bowl selection played through 1965 with the Bears and retired after one season with the Los Angeles Rams.

50
WILLIE BROWN

he week leading up to Willie Brown was never a pleasant one. Good receivers fretted and worried; great receivers studied film, looking for weaknesses they knew didn't exist. Facing Brown, one of the game's

outstanding coverage cornerbacks, was like a trip to the dentist or an IRS audit. He was a bad dream that lasted for 16 AFL/NFL seasons—four with the Denver Broncos and 12 as the unquestioned leader of a superior Oakland Raiders secondary.

The first thing you noticed was the boyish enthusiasm Brown brought to every play, a trait he complemented with size (6-1, 195), mobility and uncanny instincts. The second was the way he took charge with a subtle swagger that shook up receivers and impressed teammates who looked up to him

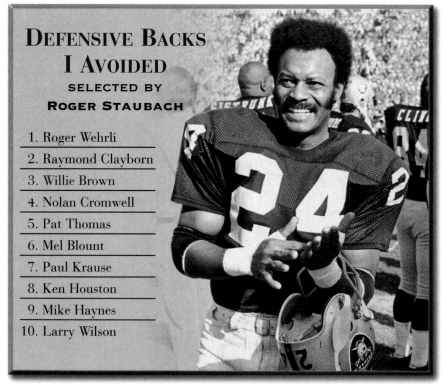

DEFENSIVE BACKS I AVOIDED

SELECTED BY ROGER STAUBACH

1. Roger Wehrli
2. Raymond Clayborn
3. Willie Brown
4. Nolan Cromwell
5. Pat Thomas
6. Mel Blount
7. Paul Krause
8. Ken Houston
9. Mike Haynes
10. Larry Wilson

some receivers and disrupted the pass patterns of others. But he also could intimidate with his ability to shadow receivers, who marveled at how he always seemed to know where they were going. A lot of it was instinct and quickness, but the hard-hitting Brown also

viewed hours of film and studied the moves and tendencies of every receiver he would face.

The incredible instinct resulted in 54 regular-season interceptions, seven more in the playoffs. One pickoff, which resulted in a 75-yard touchdown return, provided the clincher for the Raiders in a Super Bowl XI win over

as a defensive leader and guru. Brown's flamboyant, gambling style provided a stark contrast to his quiet modesty and soft, friendly off-field manner.

He always will be remembered as the man who invented the bump-and-run style that intimidated

Minnesota. It's no coincidence that in Brown's 12 seasons with Oakland, the Raiders were 128-35-7 with nine AFL/AFC championship game appearances and two Super Bowls, one a winner. He also played in nine Pro Bowls.

ALL-DECADE TEAMS

The following All-Decade Teams reflect TSN's all-stars for the 10-year periods 1920-1929, 1930-1939, 1940-1949, etc. The goal was to find the most dominant players for each position during those spans as well as the top coaches and specialists. Because of the two-way football played through the 1940s, a combined offensive/defensive team was selected for the first three decades.

1920s

QB— Paddy Driscoll
HB— Red Grange
HB— Jim Thorpe
FB— Ernie Nevers
 E— Guy Chamberlin
 E— Lavern Dilweg
 T— Wilbur Henry
 T— Roy "Link" Lyman
 G— Ed Healey
 G— Mike Michalske
 C— George Trafton
 K— Wilbur Henry
 P— Paddy Driscoll
Coach—George Halas

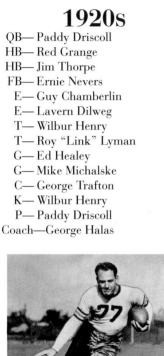

Red Grange

Mel Hein

1930s

QB— Arnie Herber
HB— Cliff Battles
HB— Johnny (Blood) McNally
FB— Bronko Nagurski
 E— Bill Hewitt
 E— Don Hutson
 T— Cal Hubbard
 T— Turk Edwards
 G— George Musso
 G— Gover "Ox" Emerson
 C— Mel Hein
 K— Earl "Dutch" Clark
 P— Clarke Hinkle
Coach—Earl "Curly" Lambeau

1940s

QB— Sammy Baugh
HB— Steve Van Buren
HB— George McAfee
FB— Marion Motley
 E— Don Hutson
 E— Dante Lavelli
 T— Frank "Bruiser" Kinard
 T— Al Wistert
 G— Bucko Kilroy
 G— Bill Willis
 C— Clyde "Bulldog" Turner
 K— Lou Groza
 P— Sammy Baugh
Coach—George Halas

Sammy Baugh

1950s

OFFENSE

QB— Otto Graham
HB— Ollie Matson
HB— Hugh McElhenny
FB— Joe Perry
 E— Pete Pihos
 E— Elroy "Crazy Legs" Hirsch
 T— Lou Creekmur
 T— Roosevelt Brown
 G— Stan Jones
 G— Dick Stanfel
 C— Chuck Bednarik

DEFENSE

 E— Gino Marchetti
 E— Len Ford
 T— Leo Nomellini
 T— Ernie Stautner
LB— Bill George
LB— Sam Huff
LB— Joe Schmidt
DB— Jack Christiansen
DB— Bobby Dillon
DB— Dick "Night Train" Lane
DB— Emlen Tunnell

K—Lou Groza
P—Horace Gillom
KR—Ollie Matson
PR—Jack Christiansen
Coach—Paul Brown

Elroy "Crazy Legs" Hirsch

1960s

OFFENSE

QB— Johnny Unitas
RB— Gale Sayers
RB— Jim Brown
WR— Lance Alworth
WR— Charley Taylor
TE— John Mackey
T— Forrest Gregg
T— Ron Mix
G— Jerry Kramer
G— Jim Parker
C— Jim Otto

DEFENSE

E— Willie Davis
E— Deacon Jones
T— Bob Lilly
T— Merlin Olsen
LB— Bobby Bell
LB— Dick Butkus
LB— Ray Nitschke
CB— Herb Adderley
CB— Willie Brown
S— Larry Wilson
S— Willie Wood

K— George Blanda
P— Jerrel Wilson
KR— Gale Sayers
PR— Speedy Duncan
Coach—Vince Lombardi

John Mackey

1970s

OFFENSE

QB— Roger Staubach
RB— Walter Payton
RB— O.J. Simpson
WR— Fred Biletnikoff
WR— Paul Warfield
TE— Dave Casper
T— Art Shell
T— Ron Yary
G— Larry Little
G— Gene Upshaw
C— Jim Langer

DEFENSE

E— Carl Eller
E— Jack Youngblood
T— Joe Greene
T— Alan Page
LB— Jack Ham
LB— Willie Lanier
LB— Jack Lambert
CB— Willie Brown
CB— Mel Blount
S— Cliff Harris
S— Ken Houston

K—Jan Stenerud, P—Ray Guy,
KR—Mercury Morris, PR—Rick
Upchurch, Coach—Don Shula

Walter Payton

1980s

K— Nick Lowery
P— Rohn Stark
KR— Dennis Gentry
PR— Billy Johnson,
Coach—Bill Walsh

Lawrence Taylor

OFFENSE

QB— Joe Montana
RB— Eric Dickerson
RB— Tony Dorsett
WR— Jerry Rice
WR— Steve Largent
TE— Kellen Winslow
T— Anthony Munoz
T— Jackie Slater
G— John Hannah
G— Bruce Matthews
C— Dwight Stephenson

DEFENSE

E— Howie Long
E— Reggie White
T— Dan Hampton
T— Randy White
LB— Mike Singletary
LB— Lawrence Taylor
LB— Harry Carson
CB— Darrell Green
CB— Mike Haynes
S— Ronnie Lott
S— Deron Cherry

1990s

OFFENSE

QB— Steve Young
RB— Barry Sanders
RB— Emmitt Smith
WR— Jerry Rice
WR— Cris Carter
TE— Shannon Sharpe
T— Bruce Armstrong
T— Richmond Webb
G— Randall McDaniel
G— Bruce Matthews
C— Dermontti Dawson

DEFENSE

E— Reggie White
E— Bruce Smith
T— Cortez Kennedy
T— John Randle
LB— Junior Seau
LB— Derrick Thomas
LB— Greg Lloyd
CB— Deion Sanders
CB— Rod Woodson
S— Steve Atwater
S— Carnell Lake

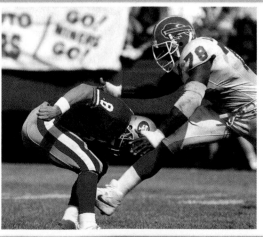

K—Morten Andersen
P—Matt Turk
KR—Mel Gray
PR—Eric Metcalf
Coach—Jimmy Johnson

Bruce Smith

"HE'S JUST MEAN. THAT'S ALL YOU CAN SAY.
HE GETS UP FOR GAMES, EVERY GAME.
OFF THE FIELD, HE'S A NICE GUY ...
ONE OF THE NICEST GUYS IN THE WORLD.
BUT HE'S MEAN OTHERWISE."

FORMER COWBOYS TEAMMATE
HARVEY MARTIN, 1980

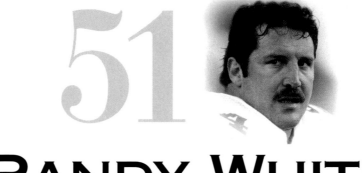

51 RANDY WHITE

They called him "Manster"—as in half-man, half-monster. Randy White didn't just beat up on offensive opponents, he destroyed them. He was a 6-4, 257-pound Jekyll-Hyde personality in a defensive tackle's body, a demon who could single-handedly dismantle game plans. To the Dallas fans he entertained every Sunday for 14 seasons, he was the second coming of Bob Lilly in the middle of the Doomsday Defense.

No right-thinking offensive coordinator could plan for Dallas without first neutralizing White, the former Outland Trophy winner from Maryland. That usually took two or three blockers—good news for other Cowboys defenders. When opponents chose instead to run away from White, which they often did, he could chase them down with his surprising lateral quickness.

Off the field, White was quiet, shy and soft-spoken, an easy-living, easy-to-like man. On the field, he was "just plain mean," a reflection of the intensity that pushed him to 100 percent effort on every play. He also was the strongest man on the Cowboys' roster, the product of his obsession with weightlifting. His strength allowed him to shed blockers with ease and his quickness allowed him to rush the passer with a stop-me-if-you-can scorn. When big No. 54 broke through the line, quarterbacks had a serious decision to make—quickly.

With White operating at peak efficiency from the right tackle slot, the Cowboys rolled to six championship game appearances and three Super Bowls from 1975 (his rookie year) through the 1982 season. The pass-rushing combination of White and end Harvey Martin was so dominant in a Super Bowl XII victory over Denver that the two shared MVP

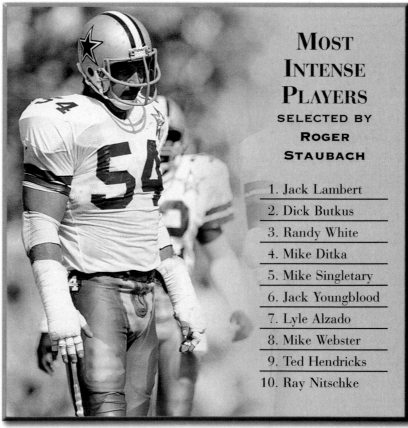

MOST INTENSE PLAYERS

SELECTED BY ROGER STAUBACH

1. Jack Lambert
2. Dick Butkus
3. Randy White
4. Mike Ditka
5. Mike Singletary
6. Jack Youngblood
7. Lyle Alzado
8. Mike Webster
9. Ted Hendricks
10. Ray Nitschke

honors—a rare honor for defensive players. Equally impressive were the string of nine Pro Bowl appearances White earned (1977-1985) and the fact he missed only one game in his career.

52

BOBBY LAYNE

He was equal parts George Patton and party animal. But whether Bobby Layne was guiding the Detroit Lions to another dramatic victory or his teammates to the nearest bar, there never was any

doubt who was in charge. Layne was the ultimate leader, a quarterback who drove the Lions to consecutive NFL championships (1952 and '53) and himself to the edge of physical endurance.

The husky, round-faced Layne swaggered through a 15-year NFL career that marked him as one of the game's most successful field generals and a relentless carouser. Layne ran a huddle like boot camp, castigating teammates for mistakes and prodding them for extra effort. He simply wouldn't tolerate losing and backed up his take-charge demeanor with clever play-calling, a reliable arm that amassed 26,768 passing yards and quick feet that ran for 2,451 yards and 25 touchdowns.

Layne, who played without a facemask, was the first acknowledged master of the two-minute drill, a talent that fit his adventurous, life-on-the-edge

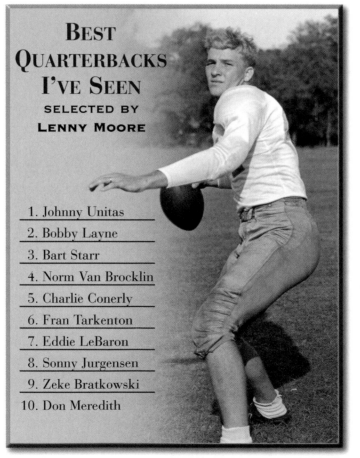

BEST QUARTERBACKS I'VE SEEN
SELECTED BY LENNY MOORE

1. Johnny Unitas
2. Bobby Layne
3. Bart Starr
4. Norm Van Brocklin
5. Charlie Conerly
6. Fran Tarkenton
7. Eddie LeBaron
8. Sonny Jurgensen
9. Zeke Bratkowski
10. Don Meredith

personality. He basked in the dramatics of a last-minute victory, then made a beeline for the nearest party, usually with his teammates in tow. Layne, complete with colorful quotes delivered in a deep Texas twang, became a legendary figure, a bigger-than-life personality during an era when pro football was groping for an identity.

While his playboy image sometimes upstaged his athletic talent, it's hard to deny Layne's football contributions. The 1952 championship broke a 16-year postseason drought for the Lions. He also led the team through most of a 1957 championship season before sitting out the title game with an ankle injury. In addition to throwing 196 TD passes, Layne kicked 34 field goals and 120 extra points over a career that included one-year stays with the Chicago Bears (1948) and New York Bulldogs (1949) and four-plus years in Pittsburgh (1958-62) to finish his career.

“HE WAS THE GREATEST TWO-MINUTE QUARTERBACK EVER. BOBBY LAYNE SIMPLY NEVER LOST A GAME. SOMETIMES, TIME JUST RAN OUT ON HIM.”

FORMER LIONS TEAMMATE
DOAK WALKER
THE SPORTING NEWS

"TONY'S A GUY WHO'S CAPABLE OF BREAKING AT ANY TIME. HE JUST HAS SUCH TREMENDOUS ACCELERATION. HE'LL SEE A NARROW ALLEY AND, SUDDENLY, BE GONE RIGHT THROUGH BEFORE YOU KNOW IT."

FORMER DALLAS COACH
TOM LANDRY, 1978
THE SPORTING NEWS

53 TONY DORSETT

A t first glance, Tony Dorsett appeared grossly overmatched in a league of behemoths. But then he tucked the ball into his muscular 5-11, 192-pound body and destroyed that myth, much like he would destroy game plans with exciting consistency over a memorable 12-year career. Touchdown Tony was a yardage-eating machine for the Dallas Cowboys, living proof that good things can come in small packages.

Dorsett, the 1976 Heisman Trophy winner who set an NCAA career rushing record at Pittsburgh, was blessed with remarkable balance and acceleration, qualities that allowed him to stop and start, dart and slash while searching for a hole. Woe to the defense that allowed him to wander along the line of scrimmage looking for daylight. Nobody could rev up to top speed faster and nobody could cut against the grain with such spectacular results.

Of Dorsett's 77 rushing touchdowns, five came on runs of 75 yards or longer. He consistently defied skeptics who thought he would wear down over time by posting eight 1,000-yard efforts in his first nine NFL seasons (only the strike-shortened 1982 season prevented a 9-for-9 mark). He also was a competent receiver, willing blocker and good team player who helped the Cowboys reach five NFC championship games and two Super Bowls, one of which produced a victory over Denver.

Dorsett's running style matched his off-field personality. He was quiet and shy when he leaned forward, looking, looking, looking for the hole. He was articulate and expressive when his big brown eyes lit up and he suddenly exploded into action. Dorsett expressed himself to the tune of 12,739 yards in regular-season play—fourth on the all-time list through 1998—and 1,383 more as one of the top postseason rushers in history. He retired as a four-time Pro Bowl selection in 1988, after a 703-yard season with the Denver Broncos.

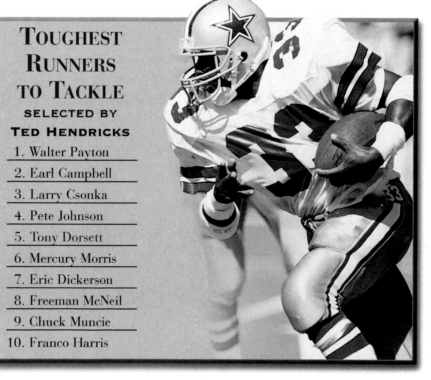

TOUGHEST RUNNERS TO TACKLE

SELECTED BY
TED HENDRICKS

1. Walter Payton
2. Earl Campbell
3. Larry Csonka
4. Pete Johnson
5. Tony Dorsett
6. Mercury Morris
7. Eric Dickerson
8. Freeman McNeil
9. Chuck Muncie
10. Franco Harris

"BEDNARIK HATES TO SEE ANYBODY STANDING UP ON THE FIELD. EVERY TIME HE DOES SEE A MAN STANDING AROUND WITH THE WHISTLE YET TO BLOW HALTING A PLAY, HE KNOCKS HIM DOWN JUST FOR THE SHEER JOY OF IT. HE'LL CHOOSE ANYBODY."

FORMER REDSKINS COACH
JOE KUHARICH, 1954

54 CHUCK BEDNARIK

The No. 60 he wore on his Philadelphia jersey was prophetic, a harbinger of his now-enduring fame as professional football's last 60-minute player and hero of the Eagles' 1960 championship game.

Chuck Bednarik was many things during his outstanding 14-year NFL career, but he'll always be remembered for the one magical season he celebrated at the not-so-tender football age of 35.

When the 1960 campaign opened, Bednarik was beginning his 12th season and sixth straight at center, after a mid-career switch from linebacker. But an injury to linebacker Bob Pellegrini in the Eagles' fifth game prompted coach Buck Shaw to ask Bednarik to revive the long-discarded concept of two-way football. The former University of Pennsylvania star played offense and defense the rest of the season and capped off his 58-minute championship game performance with a victory-saving bear-hug tackle of Green Bay's Jim Taylor at the Eagles' 10-yard line.

BEST PLAYERS I'VE SEEN
SELECTED BY PAUL WARFIELD

1. Jim Brown
2. Dick Butkus
3. Johnny Unitas
4. Jerry Rice
5. Don Hutson
6. Barry Sanders
7. Chuck Bednarik
8. Marion Motley
9. Jim Parker
10. Reggie White

Bednarik was as rugged as the Bethlehem, Pa., steel town he called home. He was an old-school competitor who threw his 6-3, 233-pound body around with reckless abandon, whether creating holes with his relentless blocking or making punishing, sometimes vicious tackles. In an era of evolving offenses, he was the perfect linebacker: big, tall and agile with the ability to cover short passes. He had a mean streak and played for keeps, prompting opponents to eye him

with understandable trepidation.

Bednarik wasn't the fastest or strongest man to play linebacker, but he more than made up for that with a tunnel-vision dedication and a great instinct for diagnosing plays. Wherever the ball was, Bednarik would be close by. And if the Eagles needed a big play, he would deliver. An eight-time Pro Bowl player, he finished his career in 1962 with a surprising total of 20 interceptions.

"HE WAS ONE OF THOSE QUIET LEADERS WHO COMMANDED RESPECT JUST BY BEING A GREAT PLAYER. HE NEVER, EVER ACTED LIKE A TOUGH GUY. HE WAS ALWAYS NICE AND BUSINESSLIKE. BUT WHETHER YOU WERE HIS TEAMMATE OR AN OPPONENT, YOU KNEW THIS WAS A MAN WHO DESERVED YOUR DEEPEST RESPECT."

FORMER RAIDERS COACH
JOHN MADDEN

55

ART SHELL

It was a fundamental rule, understood and followed by every defensive player in the NFL: Do not make Art Shell mad. The Oakland Raiders' hulking offensive tackle was intimidating enough in his "kill-you-softly,

gentlemanly" mode. Arouse the bear and pay the price—a price that was exacted over 15 superlative seasons with methodical and relentless consistency.

The quiet, introspective Shell was listed at a brutish 6-5 and 265 pounds, but the weight fluctuated as high as 310—a figure he wouldn't confirm. He never played the role of tough guy, preferring to let his strength and quickness speak for itself. He would greet opponents with flashing brown eyes, his wide, trademark smile and the words, "Let's have a great game." Then he would run them into the ground for 60 sometimes-painful minutes.

There was never anything personal with Shell. He was simply doing his job, one he took very seriously. He was extremely physical, never got rattled and knew the offensive assignments of every teammate, a result of the game film he studied for hours every night.

Shell and guard Gene Upshaw formed a dominating left side for the Raiders for 14 seasons, operating as a well-oiled machine whether run blocking or protecting the passer.

The Shell/Upshaw dominance was on display in Super Bowl XI when the Raiders rushed for 266 yards,

most of them coming over the left side against the heralded right side of the Vikings' defensive line: tackle Alan Page and end Jim Marshall. Shell spent most of

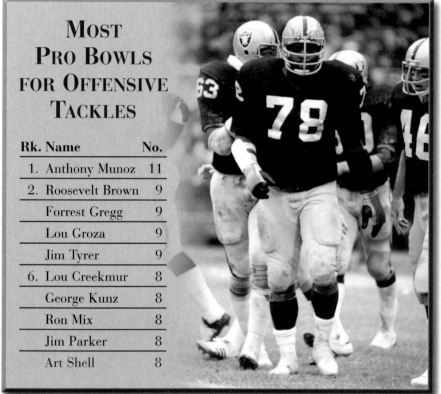

MOST PRO BOWLS FOR OFFENSIVE TACKLES

Rk.	Name	No.
1.	Anthony Munoz	11
2.	Roosevelt Brown	9
	Forrest Gregg	9
	Lou Groza	9
	Jim Tyrer	9
6.	Lou Creekmur	8
	George Kunz	8
	Ron Mix	8
	Jim Parker	8
	Art Shell	8

the game blocking Marshall and held him without a tackle—or an assist. Raiders fans became accustomed to such efforts from Shell, who helped lead the team to 11 playoff appearances, nine AFL/AFC championship game appearances and two Super Bowl wins. Shell also played in eight Pro Bowls.

56

MIKE SINGLETARY

ormer teammates remember the inspirational speeches, the fiery and demonstrative pregame diatribes that usually resulted in at least minor damage to furniture. Intensity never was a problem for Mike Singletary, who listened to Bach and Beethoven to get "pumped-down" for opponents. If success can be measured by sheer will and determination, the Chicago Bears' No. 50 could match up with anybody who ever played the middle linebacker position.

Singletary needed that kind of edge to overcome deficiencies in size (6-0, 230) and speed. What he couldn't do when he came out of Baylor University in 1981 he learned through obsessive dedication. He hated coming out of games in third-down situations so he spent countless hours after practice working on coverage techniques that eventually allowed him to become a complete player. He approached the game like a coach, studying film to learn tendencies and memorizing the nuances of every position.

Singletary, who was built like a fireplug with thick neck and a powerful upper body, was a walking contradiction. Off the field, he looked at life through thick-rimmed glasses and spoke in the soft, thoughtful tones of a high school math teacher. On the field, he was constant motion, totally focused and dedicated to getting the man with the ball. He was at his best as a run-stuffer who could throw his body into the fray with total disregard for

life or limb.

Nobody could match the relentless desire and enthusiasm that kept Singletary in the lineup for all but two games of a 12-year career. The man who was

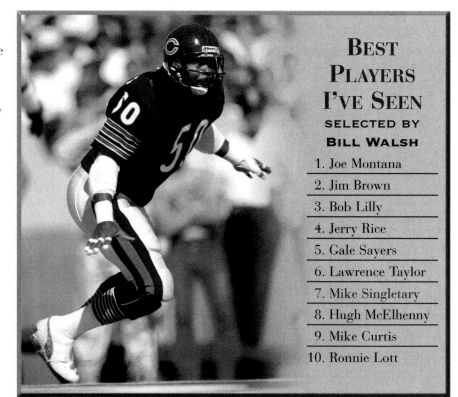

BEST PLAYERS I'VE SEEN
SELECTED BY BILL WALSH

1. Joe Montana
2. Jim Brown
3. Bob Lilly
4. Jerry Rice
5. Gale Sayers
6. Lawrence Taylor
7. Mike Singletary
8. Hugh McElhenny
9. Mike Curtis
10. Ronnie Lott

"too small and too slow" earned 10 Pro Bowl selections and acclaim as a middle linebacker in the throwback mold of Dick Butkus. Singletary's happiest moment came in 1985 when he helped the Bears complete an 18-1 season that was capped with a victory over New England in Super Bowl XX.

"I haven't seen a linebacker play with his intensity since I played with Butkus."

Former Bears defensive tackle Jim Osborne, 1986
The Sporting News

57

ROOSEVELT BROWN

The path Roosevelt Brown followed from the 27th round of the 1953 NFL draft to pro football stardom was straight and narrow, unlike the paths he cleared for New York Giants ballcarriers. He was known around football circles as a quick hitter, someone who could knock a defender off the line before he knew what was happening. Brown was Mr. Reliable over a 13-year

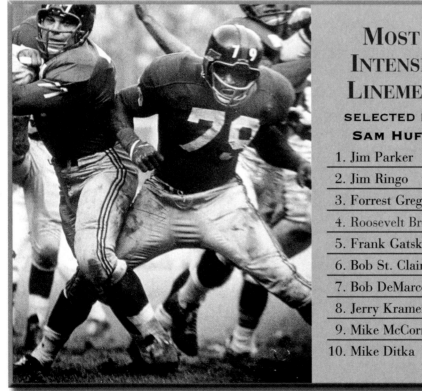

MOST INTENSE LINEMEN

SELECTED BY SAM HUFF

1. Jim Parker
2. Jim Ringo
3. Forrest Gregg
4. Roosevelt Brown
5. Frank Gatski
6. Bob St. Clair
7. Bob DeMarco
8. Jerry Kramer
9. Mike McCormack
10. Mike Ditka

upper body that could deliver punishment. But unlike most offensive linemen of the era, he had excellent straightaway speed and superior quickness.

Brown was quickly inserted into the tackle slot, a job he would hold for the rest of his career. He was too quick for the stronger defensive linemen and too persistent for anybody who tried to outmaneuver him on a pass play. He was so fast that he pulled on sweeps—one of the first tackles to be used in that manner. The Giants also utilized Brown's speed and agility on kick-coverage teams.

But Brown was valuable beyond his obvious skills and physical assets. He was very popular among teammates and inspired them with his never-give-an-inch desire and relentless determination. The Giants liked to insert him on defense for goal-line stands, a move that seemed to give the unit an emotional lift. Brown, a nine-time Pro Bowl selection, helped lift the Giants over a successful 10-year stretch (1954 to '63) in which they carved out an 86-35-5 record that produced six conference titles and one NFL championship.

career that started in the trenches and ended in the Hall of Fame.

Brown, an afterthought draft pick out of Morgan State, gained instant attention when he arrived at the Giants camp and began throwing around his 6-3, 255-pound body. He had wide shoulders and a powerful

"ROSEY NEVER DID THE SAME THINGS TWICE. HE WAS INCREDIBLE. HE WAS MY FAVORITE, MY IDOL. EVERYTHING I LEARNED, I PICKED UP FROM HIM. I WANTED TO BE JUST LIKE HIM."

JIM PARKER, 1999

58

BRUCE SMITH

It all starts with that muscular body, fine-tuned and sculpted, and tunnel-vision passion. Bruce Smith has long been consumed by an obsession to be the best defensive end in football and nothing short of perfection will be tolerated. It's an obsession that grows with every mad dash to the quarterback and run-stuffing tackle. A passion that will not go away after 14 NFL seasons as a sackmaster and difference-maker for Buffalo's long-outstanding defense.

Smith makes life miserable for offensive coordinators, who must devise complex blocking schemes to keep him out of their backfield. The 6-4, 275-pound Smith is faster than most linebackers and stronger than most 300-pounders, but it's the lightning quickness and his ability to knife through blockers at impossible angles that set him apart. When he speed-rushes around end, he looks like a skater cornering, low to the ground and almost flat—a guided missile.

The strength, massive thighs and 19-inch neck are products of an intensive workout routine that became almost obsessive after his early years as a 300-pound doughboy. Smith also worked hard to improve the mental aspects of his game, studying film to the point of exhaustion and becoming a student of opponent tendencies. Nobody is better prepared and play-by-play consistent, which explains his ability to reach double digits in sacks 12 times in 14 years.

The skills are impressive, but many opponents fall victim to the heart-stopping glare and superior, cocky attitude the former Virginia Tech star brings to the field. The only thing missing from a resume that

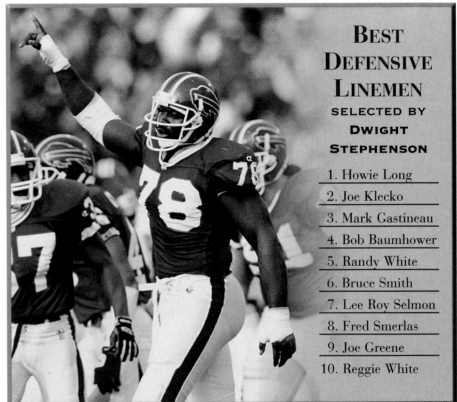

BEST DEFENSIVE LINEMEN
SELECTED BY
DWIGHT STEPHENSON

1. Howie Long
2. Joe Klecko
3. Mark Gastineau
4. Bob Baumhower
5. Randy White
6. Bruce Smith
7. Lee Roy Selmon
8. Fred Smerlas
9. Joe Greene
10. Reggie White

includes 164 sacks (second on the all-time list to Reggie White's 192½) and nine Pro Bowl selections is a championship, a frustration exacerbated by Buffalo's four straight Super Bowl losses from 1991 to '94.

"WHEN OTHER PLAYERS SAY SOMETHING
(COCKY), IT'S LIP SERVICE. THEY KNOW DEEP
DOWN THAT THEY HAVE LIMITATIONS. BUT NOT
BRUCE SMITH. HE KNOWS HE CAN BE THE
GREATEST WHO HAS EVER PLAYED THIS GAME."

FORMER BILLS DEFENSIVE LINE COACH
CHUCK DICKERSON, 1991
TSN PRO FOOTBALL YEARBOOK

"I NEVER SAW A QUARTERBACK
WHO COULD DO IT SO MANY WAYS,
AND WHO WORKED SO HARD AT IT.
HE WILL BE KNOWN AS THE
GREATEST QUARTERBACK BY THE
TIME HE FINISHES. I DON'T KNOW
IF ANYBODY ELSE WILL BE CLOSE."

FORMER VIKINGS COACH
BUD GRANT, 1976

59
FRAN TARKENTON

Off the field, Fran Tarkenton was a Boy Scout athlete, the articulate, straight-arrow son of a Methodist minister. On the field, he was a daring, improvising, scrambling 190-pound quarterback who played Russian roulette with 270-pound defensive linemen. He was a novelty in the 1960s, a record-setting star in the '70s. During an 18-year NFL career that propelled him to the top of

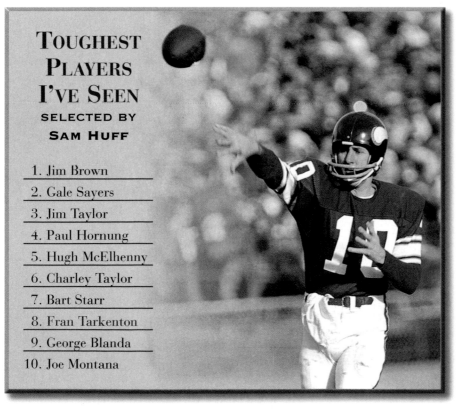

TOUGHEST PLAYERS I'VE SEEN
SELECTED BY SAM HUFF

1. Jim Brown
2. Gale Sayers
3. Jim Taylor
4. Paul Hornung
5. Hugh McElhenny
6. Charley Taylor
7. Bart Starr
8. Fran Tarkenton
9. George Blanda
10. Joe Montana

ran for his life from giants who were bent on destruction but gasping for the fortitude to continue their chase. Every game against Tarkenton was exhausting, a defensive marathon. He flitted around the field like a butterfly, a startling departure from the era's dropback passers who stood bravely in the pocket.

The catch-me-if-you-can style was a product of Tarkenton's uncanny sixth sense, quick feet and ability to throw accurately on the run. His arm was not strong, but he had great touch. His scrambles were not planned but often created big plays. There was no way to defend against the offensive fireworks Tarkenton was capable of setting off.

For his first 11 seasons with weak Minnesota and New York Giants teams, Tarkenton was simply a quarterback. For his last seven with the beefed-up Vikings, he was a consummate field general capable of generating lots of points. From 1973

every major passing chart, Tarkenton revolutionized the way the quarterback position was played.

Tark's 1961 debut season with the expansion Minnesota Vikings served notice to defenders throughout the league. He darted, turned, juked and

to '78, he led the Vikings to six straight NFC Central titles and three Super Bowls, all losses. The nine-time Pro Bowl selection retired at age 38 with 47,003 passing yards and 342 touchdown passes, a figure that still ranks No. 2 on the all-time list.

60

PAUL WARFIELD

Paul Warfield's pass routes weren't diagrammed; they were choreographed. His graceful, prancing style seemed more appropriate for a ballet than a football field. He jigged. He jagged. A quick cut left, a fake right, then whoosh! He was gone. For 13 NFL seasons with Cleveland and Miami, Warfield danced his way through secondaries and into the hearts of appreciative fans.

The misfortune of Paul Warfield is that he never got a chance to play in a passing offense. His sprinter's speed, magic moves, soft hands and elusive running ability could have garnered huge numbers in a vertical attack. But the Browns (1964-69, 1976-77) and Dolphins (1970-74) were winning division titles and championships with run-oriented systems that benefited greatly from Warfield's presence as a constant home run threat.

The numbers tell the story. Warfield's 427 career receptions netted 8,565 yards and an all-time record average of 20.1. His ratio of one touchdown per 5.0 catches ranks second all-time to Don Hutson's ratio of one TD per 4.9 receptions. Warfield was dangerous at all times and demanded constant double-team attention, which kept teams from stacking the line. But he was used more often as a blocker, a job the 6-0, 188-pounder handled with surprising efficiency.

Shy and introverted, Warfield handled his plight without complaint. Despite his limited role, he was a big fan favorite with the Browns, who posted a 59-23-2 record over his first six seasons while winning one NFL championship. The Dolphins were 57-12-1 with consecutive Super Bowl winners and three AFC

BEST PLAYERS I'VE SEEN

SELECTED BY CHARLIE JOINER

1. Jim Brown
2. Gale Sayers
3. Paul Warfield
4. Deacon Jones
5. Joe Greene
6. Dick Butkus
7. Johnny Unitas
8. Willie Davis
9. Buck Buchanan
10. Willie Brown

championships during Warfield's five seasons. But Miami ran 70 percent of the time during its perfect 1972 campaign and Warfield caught only 29 passes. He caught as many as 50 passes only twice.

But his efforts did not go unnoticed: Warfield was elected to eight Pro Bowls in a career that ended in 1977 after a two-year return stint with Cleveland.

61
KEN HOUSTON

onsistency. Game after game, season after season, that quality separated Ken Houston from the crowd. As a 14-year strong safety for the Houston Oilers and Washington Redskins, he efficiently

provided a last line of defense with his special knack for being in the right place at the right time.

Houston's greatest talent might have been the instinct that helped him make intelligent decisions. But he also was blessed with excellent quickness and speed, the product of strong legs that carried his sinewy 6-3, 197-pound body around the field with long, fluid strides. Houston, a former college linebacker, was a punishing hitter when supporting on the run, a cunning blitzer and a first-class ballhawk who was especially dangerous on interception returns.

Of his 49 career interceptions (for 898 yards), a record nine were returned for touchdowns, including four in 1971 when he also returned a fumble for an Oilers TD. He also was durable, an iron man who

SAFETIES I MOST ADMIRE
SELECTED BY RONNIE LOTT

1. Jack Tatum	6. Jake Scott
2. Kenny Easley	7. Donnie Shell
3. Paul Krause	8. Dick LeBeau
4. Ken Houston	9. George Atkinson
5. Larry Wilson	10. Carnell Lake

played in 183 straight games before a broken arm ended his 1979 season with Washington. Though Houston's performance often escaped the notice of fans, coaches and teammates marveled at his unwavering work ethic and the consistency with which he graded out on film.

It was the same consistency he brought to his personal life, which he dedicated to charity work in the Houston area. Houston, who was selected to 12 Pro Bowls, spent his first six seasons (1967 to '72) with Houston before the rebuilding Oilers traded him to Washington, where he became a captain and defensive signal-caller. The only thing missing from Houston's resume was a championship, though he was a member of the Oilers team that lost to Oakland in the 1967 AFL title game.

"HOW MANY TIMES DO YOU HAVE A CHANCE TO WATCH THE BEST THERE EVER WAS AT A POSITION? MANY TOWNS ARE NEVER BLESSED LIKE THAT. YOU ONLY READ ABOUT THE GREAT ONES OR SEE THEM ONCE IN A WHILE. BUT WASHINGTON FANS HAVE HAD EIGHT YEARS TO STUDY AND APPRECIATE KENNY."

FORMER REDSKINS COACH
GEORGE ALLEN, 1980

"ANY TIME YOU COME INTO
AN ORGANIZATION AS A ROOKIE, YOU START
ALL BUT ONE GAME FOR THE NEXT 15
YEARS, YOUR TEAM GOES TO THE SUPER
BOWL IN YOUR FIRST YEAR AND THEN TWO
MORE TIMES, YOU PLAY WITH SOME OF
THE GREATEST PLAYERS WHO EVER PLAYED
THE GAME AND YOU RISE ABOVE AT LEAST
95 PERCENT OF THEM—YOU'VE
ACCOMPLISHED SOMETHING REMARKABLE."

RAIDERS OWNER AL DAVIS

62

GENE UPSHAW

I t was a religious experience, a broom-waving moment for Oakland fans. Big No. 63 would step back at the snap, move laterally to his left and sprint ahead of a Raiders ball-toting convoy. First a defensive back would show up on Gene Upshaw's radar screen, then a linebacker—targets for annihilation. Then a bulldozing block would send bodies flying and clear the way for another successful power sweep.

Upshaw was Oakland's Big Sweeper and masterful left guard for 15 seasons, a line fixture from the 1967 day he was drafted out of Texas A&I by Al Davis. Upshaw was targeted for guard, even though his 6-5, 255-pound body was much bigger than the fire-plug-like players who traditionally manned the position. Davis was looking for somebody who could block monster Kansas City tackle Buck Buchanan (6-7, 270) and their one-on-one battles became football classics.

The intelligent, intense and always-dedicated Upshaw was equally proficient as a straight-ahead blocker or pass blocker, a 14-year linemate of Hall of Fame left tackle Art Shell. He also was a team leader, coach John Madden's choice as offensive captain in 1969—his third NFL season. Upshaw provided a liaison between an admiring Davis and the team's players, who looked to him for advice. His intelligence carried over to the way he consistently approached his work.

The mild-mannered Upshaw could knock over writers with his enormous black eyes and thunderous laughter, or the body-pounding Upshaw could knock over defenders with his savage blocks. It's no coincidence that the Raiders won the AFL championship in his rookie season and two Super Bowls before he retired after the 1981 season. They also reached the AFL/AFC championship game 10 times. The seven-time Pro Bowl selection started 207 straight games before the streak ended in his final season.

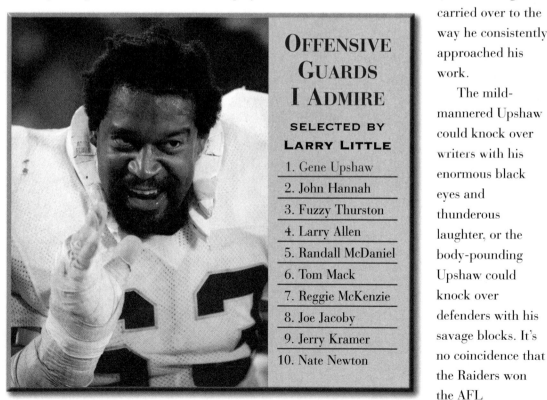

OFFENSIVE GUARDS I ADMIRE

SELECTED BY LARRY LITTLE

1. Gene Upshaw
2. John Hannah
3. Fuzzy Thurston
4. Larry Allen
5. Randall McDaniel
6. Tom Mack
7. Reggie McKenzie
8. Joe Jacoby
9. Jerry Kramer
10. Nate Newton

63 STEVE YOUNG

The first problem for defenses is a rifle left arm that can pick them apart with deadly accuracy. But don't forget the powerful legs that keep Steve Young out of harm's way and break the will of frustrated opponents at crucial moments. He's unpredictable, explosive and a threat from anywhere on the field. When Young touches the ball, good things usually happen for the San Francisco 49ers.

The 6-2, 205-pound Young is a perfect fit for the complex West Coast offense. He is resourceful, intelligent and fearless, willing to take a hit or deliver one at the end of a death-defying scramble. The seven-time Pro Bowl selection is relentlessly selective and accurate, whether patiently moving the offense with short, quick-hitting passes or hitting Jerry Rice on a deep post route.

When all else fails, it's not uncommon to see those long legs churning furiously toward daylight, with half the defense in futile pursuit. If Young isn't the most dangerous scrambler in NFL history, he's close. There's no question he's the most accurate passer ever, based on his 97.6 passer rating and .645 completion percentage through the 1998 season. And there's no doubt about a big-play ability that has delivered 229 touchdown passes, as many as 36 in one season, and two 4,000-yard campaigns.

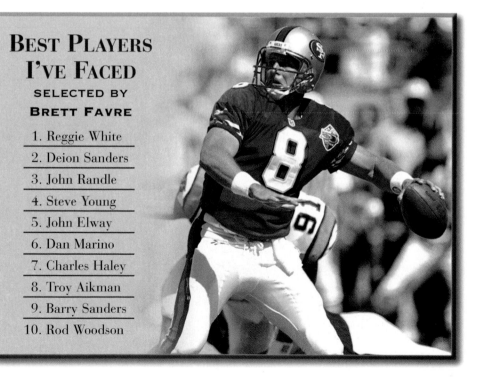

BEST PLAYERS I'VE FACED

SELECTED BY
BRETT FAVRE

1. Reggie White
2. Deion Sanders
3. John Randle
4. Steve Young
5. John Elway
6. Dan Marino
7. Charles Haley
8. Troy Aikman
9. Barry Sanders
10. Rod Woodson

Young also has delivered a Super Bowl victory with the same flair Joe Montana did throughout the 1980s. Young, a 15-year veteran who became the 49ers' full-time starter in 1991 after backing up Montana for four seasons, fired a Super Bowl-record six TD passes in the 49ers' 49-26 victory over San Diego in 1995. It was a coming-of-age performance for the charismatic Young, who languished for two seasons in the now-defunct USFL and for two more with Tampa Bay before moving to San Francisco.

"At least once a game (Hendricks) will do something and I won't know how he did it."

Former Raiders defensive coach Charlie Sumner

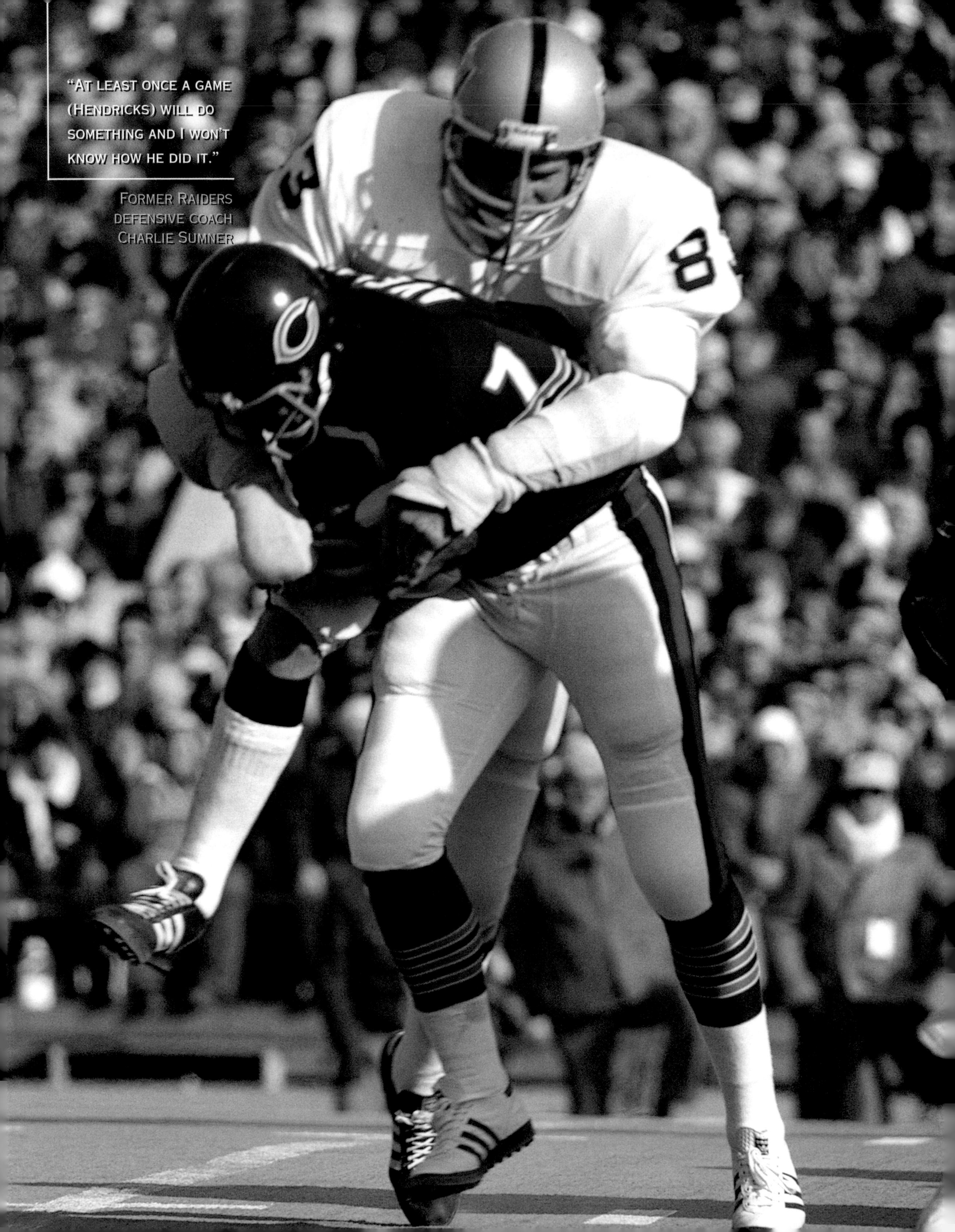

64
TED HENDRICKS

S ome said he was too tall. Others said he was too light. Everybody agreed that the 6-7, 220-pound body Ted Hendricks brought to the field was a little unorthodox for pro football. Everybody, that is, except the

Mad Stork himself, who spent 15 seasons making big plays and defying critics as one of the top outside linebackers in the game's history.

The image of a tall, flailing Hendricks rushing quarterbacks, leaping high to knock down passes, blocking kicks and wrapping his python-like arms around ballcarriers became a football fixture from 1969 to 1983, first with the Baltimore Colts, then with the Green Bay Packers and Oakland/Los Angeles Raiders. He was at his disruptive best over nine seasons with the Raiders, who gave him the freedom to roam the line, blitz on impulse, read the play and react. Nobody could key on him.

And few players could block him. Though he looked skinny, he was really a well-muscled physical specimen who

combined surprising speed with agility. His height was a major passing-lane obstacle for quarterbacks and his long arms pulled down errant passes (26 career interceptions) with amazing grace and made him the most feared kick-blocker of his era.

The on-field disruption that Hendricks wreaked was a product of the free-spirit personality that entertained teammates throughout the week and confounded more than one coach. You never knew what to expect from the Guatemala-born star, who was a curious blend of thoughtful intelligence and devil-may-care recklessness. But what you could count on was the game-day dedication and winning attitude that contributed to four Super Bowl wins (three with the Raiders, one with the Colts) and eight Pro Bowl selections— at least one with each of his teams.

LINEBACKERS I MOST ADMIRE
SELECTED BY JACK HAM

1. Andy Russell	6. Bobby Bell
2. Jack Lambert	7. Dick Butkus
3. Ted Hendricks	8. Willie Lanier
4. Lawrence Taylor	9. Dave Wilcox
5. Carl Banks	10. Mike Singletary

65

JOE SCHMIDT

It was hard not to notice Joe Schmidt, whose 18-inch neck, 48-inch barrel chest and concrete-block shoulders dominated a stocky 220-pound frame. He was the guy in the middle of the defense firing obscenities at teammates, trying to throw them into a rage before every snap; the guy standing in the wagon, whipping his team of horses. Schmidt was to the Detroit Lions' defense what Bobby Layne was to the offense— the quarterback and unquestioned field general.

Schmidt was a perfect fit for his role as one of the game's first middle linebackers. He had surprising speed with sideline-to-sideline mobility, the strength to fight off bigger offensive linemen and the ability to read plays and react with lightning-quick accuracy. Schmidt might have appeared to play at the boiling point, but his fury was controlled and his instinct for the ball remarkable. He was a serious captain who studied opponents with religious fervor.

The intangibles came as a surprise to the Lions, who grabbed the Pittsburgh star with a seventh-round pick in 1953. But he quickly drew notice as a punishing tackler while playing outside linebacker and his ball-hounding abilities surfaced when he moved to the middle in 1955. Schmidt's ability to drop into pass coverage took pressure off a quality Lions secondary that included Jack Christiansen and Yale Lary. Conversely, their coverage abilities allowed Schmidt to take intelligent gambles.

With Schmidt forming the heart of a big-play defense, Detroit rolled to NFL championships in 1953 and 1957 and fell one game short in 1954. He continued calling signals for the Lions until he ended his 13-year career after the 1965 season. When he

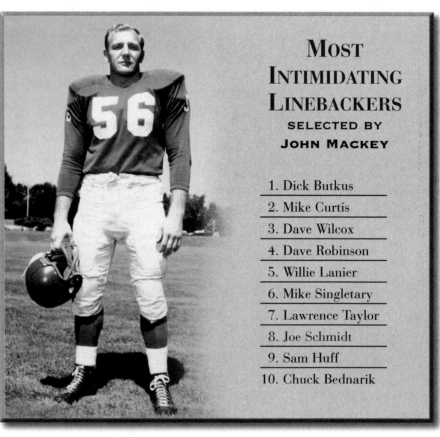

MOST INTIMIDATING LINEBACKERS
SELECTED BY JOHN MACKEY

1. Dick Butkus
2. Mike Curtis
3. Dave Wilcox
4. Dave Robinson
5. Willie Lanier
6. Mike Singletary
7. Lawrence Taylor
8. Joe Schmidt
9. Sam Huff
10. Chuck Bednarik

retired, Schmidt had produced 24 interceptions, made the Pro Bowl nine times and earned undying acclaim as one of the most beloved sports heroes in Detroit history.

"THIS GUY IS THE BEST ALL-AROUND FOOTBALL PLAYER I EVER SAW. HE CAN THROW A FOOTBALL 80 YARDS. HE CAN CENTER THE BALL BACK FARTHER AND MORE ACCURATELY THAN ANYONE IN THE BUSINESS. HE'S THE FASTEST RUNNER YOU'LL EVER SEE. HE CAN BLOCK. AND HE'S THE BEST DEFENSIVE END, CORNER LINEBACKER AND ANYTHING ELSE DEFENSIVELY IN THE WHOLE UNIVERSE."

BUCK BUCHANAN

66 BOBBY BELL

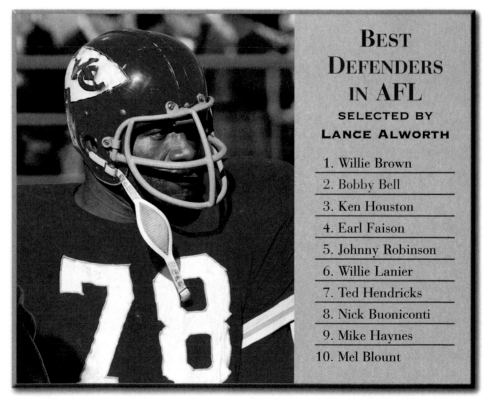

BEST DEFENDERS IN AFL
SELECTED BY
LANCE ALWORTH

1. Willie Brown
2. Bobby Bell
3. Ken Houston
4. Earl Faison
5. Johnny Robinson
6. Willie Lanier
7. Ted Hendricks
8. Nick Buoniconti
9. Mike Haynes
10. Mel Blount

He was a halfback and all-state quarterback in a dazzling high school career in Shelby, N.C. He started at the University of Minnesota as a quarterback and finished as an All-American offensive and defensive tackle. As a professional, Bobby Bell carved his Hall of Fame niche as a defensive end, outside linebacker and deep-snapper on punts and kicks.

"Bobby is the most versatile athlete I ever coached," said former Kansas City Chiefs coach Hank Stram, who claimed the 6-4, 228-pound Bell was big enough, strong enough and fast enough to play any of the 22 positions—and play them well. When Stram and the Chiefs landed Bell in the 1963 draft, the only question was how best to use the perfectly sculpted, ferocious defensive weapon they were about to unleash.

As a first-time defensive end, Bell quickly developed into one of the most feared pass rushers in the AFL. In his second year, he earned all-league honors and began stepping back as a fourth linebacker in Stram's innovative third-down "stack defense." When Stram moved him to outside linebacker in 1966, Bell began a six-year run as either an All-AFL or All-NFL performer, cementing his legacy as the first outside linebacker to gain election to the Hall.

Bell combined with linebacking mates Willie Lanier and Jim Lynch for a Kansas City team that won one of two Super Bowl appearances. He seemed to be everywhere, whether chasing down ballcarriers with cat-like quickness, thrusting aside double-team blockers with lineman-like strength or covering receivers with superior speed. He dealt out tremendous punishment and had the knack for making big plays. His 26 career interceptions resulted in runbacks totaling 479 yards (an average of 18.4) and six touchdowns.

"I WAS BIG, BUT BUCK
WAS BIGGER AND STRONGER.
YOU DON'T IMAGINE THAT A GUY
THAT BIG CAN BE SO QUICK.
OTHER GUYS I ENJOYED PLAYING
AGAINST, BUT WHEN YOU FACED
BUCHANAN, YOU COULDN'T SLEEP
THE NIGHT BEFORE THE GAME."

GENE UPSHAW

67

BUCK BUCHANAN

The sight was unnerving, like a Volkswagen going nose-to-nose with a bulldozer. There was 6-7 Buck Buchanan, his 270 pounds tucked into a three-point stance, exploding into an overmatched guard and crunching him to the ground before bouncing away in hot pursuit of the football. The size and power were bad enough. The speed, quickness and agility with which the Kansas City Chiefs' huge defensive tackle terrorized opponents for 13 seasons were another matter altogether.

Nobody had ever seen such a complete blend of physical abilities in a tall frame, much less tried to block such a force. So Chiefs coach Hank Stram changed the course of defensive line play by unleashing his monster on the suddenly undersized offensive lines of 1963. Not only did the Chiefs have a potent run-stuffer and speedy pursuer in the interior of their defense, they had one of the game's best pass rushers, all 6-7 of him, crashing right up the middle.

The emergence of the hard-working, always-friendly Buchanan, who evolved from a raw-power tackle into a smart, technically advanced defender, forced other teams to take quick action. Raiders boss Al Davis drafted 6-5, 255-pound guard Gene Upshaw with the express purpose of neutralizing Buchanan, but even the future Hall of Famer had trouble dealing with the quickness. "I'd go at him and it was like hitting a ghost," Upshaw said. And once

through the line, Buchanan could either bat down passes with his long arms or drop the quarterback.

Buchanan became the anchor and co-captain for an outstanding Chiefs defense that lost in the

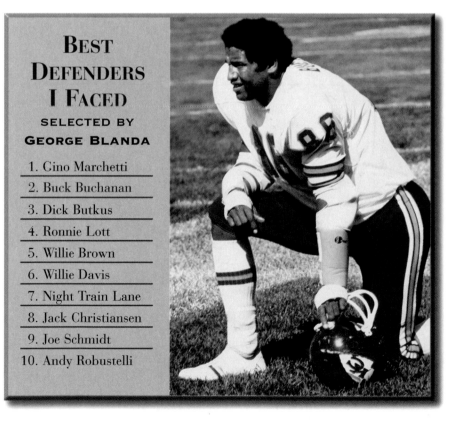

BEST DEFENDERS I FACED

SELECTED BY GEORGE BLANDA

1. Gino Marchetti
2. Buck Buchanan
3. Dick Butkus
4. Ronnie Lott
5. Willie Brown
6. Willie Davis
7. Night Train Lane
8. Jack Christiansen
9. Joe Schmidt
10. Andy Robustelli

first Super Bowl and came back three years later to upset Minnesota in Super Bowl IV. The eight-time Pro Bowl selection, who was credited with the first Super Bowl sack, missed only one game before retiring in 1975.

"Emmitt is a great player in a great system, a system that suits him perfectly. He is a hell of a warrior, and he fits the Dallas scheme better than anybody."

Jim Brown, 1997
TSN Pro Football
Yearbook

68

EMMITT SMITH

His running style is an extension of his personality—straight-ahead, no-nonsense with uncompromising dedication to the ultimate goal. When Emmitt Smith tucks the ball into his 5-9, 203-pound hard body, the shortest point to the end zone is a straight line through the middle. He's a warrior, the most prolific touchdown rusher in NFL history and the muscle behind three Dallas Cowboys Super Bowl championships in the 1990s.

It's not that Smith can't freeze defenders with quick feet and heart-stopping moves when he wants. He just prefers the grinding style, which suits the tree-trunk thighs and powerful hips that define his reputation as one of the great second-effort runners in NFL history. Smith has been a perfect match for the Cowboys' system since his arrival as the 17th pick in the 1990 draft. Operating behind a first-class line, he gets the tough yardage, the key first down when everything is on the line and first call when the Cowboys reach the red zone.

The greatness of Smith can be measured by the record 125 touchdowns he has scored on the ground, but his contributions don't stop in the end zone. He also is an outstanding blocker and reliable receiver who knows how to position himself as a bail-out option for quarterback Troy Aikman. He is a by-the-book performer who rarely deviates from the appointed hole and has been a durable, anything-for-the-team mechanic.

Smith, who has posted eight straight 1,000-yard seasons and 12,566 rushing yards, is likely to move into third place on the all-time list in 1999 behind Walter Payton and Barry Sanders. But it's more likely

TOUGHEST RUNNERS TO TACKLE
SELECTED BY **MERLIN OLSEN**

1. Jim Brown
2. Jim Taylor
3. Barry Sanders
4. Gale Sayers
5. Earl Campbell
6. Walter Payton
7. O.J. Simpson
8. Eric Dickerson
9. Terrell Davis
10. Emmitt Smith

Smith, a seven-time Pro Bowl selection and four-time rushing champ, will be more interested in obtaining a fourth Super Bowl ring and claiming a second Super Bowl MVP award.

"DAVIS IS A GREAT
PASS RUSHER.
HE'S STRONG
AND AGGRESSIVE.
HE'S ALWAYS
TOWERING OVER
YOU, COMING,
COMING ALL
THE TIME."

FORMER GIANTS
QUARTERBACK
Y.A. TITTLE

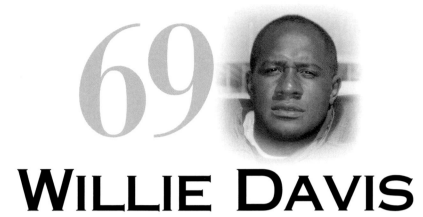

69
WILLIE DAVIS

I t was impossible not to notice Willie Davis. He had a special knack for being in the wrong place at the right time—wrong for opponents, right for Vince Lombardi's Green Bay Packers. In an era when defensive ends were seldom

seen and heard, Big Willie grabbed the spotlight with a big-play flair that contributed to the most prolific championship run in NFL history.

Davis was unusually fast for a man 6-3, 243 pounds, and he could beat offensive tackles with a bull rush, explode past them off the snap or throw them aside with quick, powerful hands. He was a rock on the Packers' impenetrable front wall and the worst nightmare for overly patient quarterbacks. Davis also was a focused, dedicated competitor who never took a game—or a play—off over his 12-season, 162-game career.

Lombardi loved the consistency his former Grambling star provided game after game, play after play, but he also loved the intelligence that allowed Davis to diagnose game situations and make quick decisions that often resulted in sack or fumbles. He was relentless, whether fighting through a pass block or pursuing a speedy ballcarrier. The gregarious, affable Davis chased down quarterbacks on Sundays

and a master's degree in business administration in his spare time.

As the Packers rolled to five NFL championships and wins in the first two Super Bowls in a seven-year stretch in the '60s, Davis became a symbol of their success—classy and unstoppable. It was an impressive

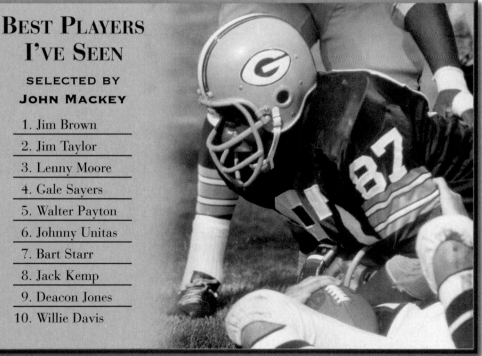

BEST PLAYERS I'VE SEEN

SELECTED BY JOHN MACKEY

1. Jim Brown
2. Jim Taylor
3. Lenny Moore
4. Gale Sayers
5. Walter Payton
6. Johnny Unitas
7. Bart Starr
8. Jack Kemp
9. Deacon Jones
10. Willie Davis

plateau for Davis, who started his career in Cleveland as a 15th-round draft pick. When he retired after the 1969 season with five Pro Bowl selections, he had recovered 21 opponents' fumbles—a team record that still stands.

Forget the smile and ever-cheerful demeanor Emlen Tunnell brought to his job. There really was a scheming con man, master thief and destructive weapon rolled into that innocent-looking 6-1, 187-pound body. The zest and abandon that made him the most popular player in the locker room for 14 NFL seasons also fueled his rise to Hall of Fame recognition as one of the greatest defensive backs and kick returners.

An undrafted Iowa standout who paid his way to New York in 1948 and asked the Giants for a tryout, Tunnell became one of the first defense-only stars of the game. Tunnell was the first black player in the Giants' post-World War II era and went on to distinction as the NFL's first black assistant coach and pro football's first black Hall of Famer. He is credited with developing many of the pass-coverage techniques for the safety position.

Emlen the Gremlin was an interception waiting to happen. He would lull quarterbacks into a sense of security and then zip into the path of the ball. Some of his 79 career interceptions (No. 2 all-time) could be

return man. He was labeled "offense on defense," a monicker he justified with 4,706 combined career yards on interception runbacks, punt returns and kickoff returns. Tunnell, who played on one championship team in New York and another in his career-ending 1961 season in Green Bay, was selected to nine Pro Bowls.

BEST 1-ON-1 TACKLERS
SELECTED BY LENNY MOORE

1. Night Train Lane
2. Emlen Tunnell
3. Joe Schmidt
4. Bill George
5. Dick Butkus
6. Ray Nitschke
7. Chuck Bednarik
8. Jack Christiansen
9. Sam Huff
10. Erich Barnes

attributed to catlike reactions, but many were the result of his free-lancing instincts and ability to read plays. Tunnell became the centerpiece for the Giants' famed "Umbrella Defense" that revolutionized defensive play by dropping linebackers into pass coverage.

But Tunnell was at his dangerous best when he dropped back to receive punts, a job he fearlessly performed 258 times as the NFL's first great punt-

70

EMLEN TUNNELL

"HE HAD BRAINS.
HE KNEW WHAT WAS
GOING ON OUT THERE.
HE COULD COVER,
TACKLE, DO IT ALL.
HE WAS SO
KNOWLEDGEABLE
ABOUT THE POSITION
AND THE DEFENSIVE
SCHEMES HE PLAYED
IN."

RAYMOND BERRY,
1999

71
LENNY MOORE

"A TACKLER JUST NEVER GETS A GOOD SHOT.
HIS FEET GO UP AND DOWN SO FAST YOU CAN
HARDLY SEE THEM HIT THE GROUND."

FORMER COLTS DEFENSIVE END
GINO MARCHETTI, 1964
THE SPORTING NEWS

Now you see him, now you don't. That was the magic of Lenny Moore, who bobbed, dipped, weaved and twisted his way through NFL defenses for 12 successful seasons. The speedy Rocket was a master of deception, whether taking a handoff or catching a pass from Baltimore quarterback Johnny Unitas—a combination that cut a swath through the team's record books from 1956 through '67.

At first sight, Moore was an unlikely candidate to cut swaths through anything. He stood 6-1 and carried 191 pounds on spindly legs that looked like they might snap at first contact. But the body proved to be as solid as the yardage totals he would pile up—first as a combination flanker/halfback and later as a runner who could catch passes out of the backfield. He finished his career with 12,393 combined yards (running, receiving and returns) and 113 touchdowns, which ranked second only to Jim Brown's 126 for a number of years.

The secret to Moore's durability was a shifty, jitterbug running style that kept tacklers from making solid contact. He would catch slants from Unitas, make two or three lightning-quick moves and end up with another big gainer. Or he could go deep with his sprinter-like speed, a threat that complemented Raymond Berry's talents as a possession receiver. As a

BEST PLAYERS I'VE SEEN
SELECTED BY HERB ADDERLEY

1. Jim Brown
2. Paul Hornung
3. Johnny Unitas
4. Lenny Moore
5. Joe Montana
6. Big Daddy Lipscomb
7. Willie Wood
8. Reggie White
9. Forrest Gregg
10. Randy Moss

halfback, he would dart into the line, legs always pumping, and suddenly break free, like a spider going in 10 different directions.

Moore, who was called "Spats" because of the way he taped his high-top shoes, enjoyed his best season in 1958, when he totaled 1,536 rushing-receiving yards and 14 touchdowns for the NFL-champion Colts. The seven-time Pro Bowl selection came back in 1964 to score 20 TDs, 16 on the ground.

"Cerebral player with modest speed, ordinary body and intuitive moves" —the scouting report on Marcus Allen was enough to put any defender to sleep. Then the real Allen would go off like an alarm clock, a sound that exhilarated Los Angeles and Kansas City fans for 16 NFL seasons. He was the classic overachiever, the man who could make you scratch your head when final numbers were added up—numbers that proved he was one of the great running backs in football history.

A 6-2, 210-pound former Heisman Trophy winner (1981), Allen was a sometimes-elusive, sometimes-overpowering runner who seemed to flow through the line, slashing and angling his body through crevices that only he could see. His timing was impeccable, as was his ability to read blocks and make the perfect cut to daylight. Once through a hole, his great vision allowed him to avoid potential pursuit avenues.

The key was a football intelligence and understanding that permitted Allen to elevate his physical talents. He knew the job of every player on offense, he could consistently outthink opponents and he was consumed with the idea of getting the maximum out of his abilities. He also was versatile—a first-rate runner, blocker and receiver and a master of the halfback pass.

Most of all, the quietly charismatic Allen was clutch—a back who always could deliver the first down and points in the red zone. Over 11 seasons with the Raiders and five with the Chiefs, he became football's first 10,000/5,000 man (12,243 rushing yards, 5,411 receiving) and scored 145 touchdowns, second to Jerry Rice on the all-time chart. He also was named Super Bowl XVIII MVP after rushing for 191 yards and scoring two touchdowns in the Raiders' victory over Washington. Allen, who helped the Chiefs reach the AFC title game after the 1993 season, was a six-time Pro Bowl selection.

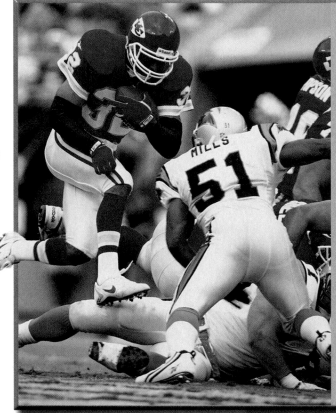

TOUGHEST RUNNERS TO TACKLE

SELECTED BY LEM BARNEY

1. Earl Campbell
2. Eric Dickerson
3. Mack Herron
4. Tony Dorsett
5. Marcus Allen
6. Barry Sanders
7. O.J. Simpson
8. Chuck Foreman
9. Terrell Davis
10. John Riggins

72
MARCUS ALLEN

"MARCUS IS A CARBON COPY OF JUICE. I'VE NEVER SEEN ANYBODY SO CLOSE TO O.J. I'M TALKING ABOUT EVERYTHING—SPEECH, MANNERISMS, THE EASE WITH WHICH HE DEALS WITH PEOPLE, TOUGHNESS, HIS WHOLE APPROACH TO THE GAME. THE TALENT IS HIS OWN, BUT IT'S UNCANNY THE WAY HE REMINDS ME OF O.J."

FORMER RAIDERS RECEIVER
BOB CHANDLER, 1982

73

KELLEN WINSLOW

Miami coach Don Shula once called him "Superman." Former San Diego quarterback Dan Fouts described him as the finest tight end ever to play the game. Kellen Winslow inspired such exultations from those who watched him perform for nine outstanding seasons in a Hall of Fame career that was cut short by a knee injury.

Critics argued that Winslow was really a wide receiver disguised as a tight end, a beneficiary of the wide-open passing offense constructed by Chargers coach Don Coryell. He would sometimes split wide as a third receiver or go in motion. Other times he would line up in the slot. He always was one of three primary receivers for Fouts and a member of prolific pass-catching trios that included Charlie Joiner and, initially, John Jefferson, then Wes Chandler.

Winslow did not revolutionize the tight end position so much as he took it to a different level. At 6-5 and 251 pounds, he provided an inviting target and his strong, springy legs allowed him to catch passes over smaller defenders. But what separated Winslow from his tight end predecessors was his big, soft hands and deceptive speed, which was a product of his long "elephant stride." His pass-catching proficiency opened eyes in 1980 when he led NFL receivers with 89 catches (then a record for a tight end) for 1,290 yards and followed that with a league-leading 88 for 1,075 yards in 1981.

The former Missouri All-American quickly became the yardstick for the pass-catching tight end. His 13-catch, 166-yard effort in the Chargers' epic playoff victory over Miami in January 1982 inspired Shula's appraisal and he caught five TD passes in a 1981 game against the Oakland Raiders. The articulate, outspoken Winslow, who played in five Pro Bowls, finished his career in 1987 with 541 catches for 6,741 yards.

BEST TIGHT ENDS
SELECTED BY JACK HAM

Russ Francis	John Mackey
Kellen Winslow	Mike Ditka
Charle Young	Jay Novacek
Ozzie Newsome	Charlie Sanders
Dave Casper	Bob Trumpy

"I DON'T KNOW WHAT IT'S LIKE TO BE MAGIC JOHNSON THROWING THE BALL IN TO KAREEM, BUT I KNOW KAREEM DOESN'T DROP MANY. THROWING TO KELLEN OVER THE MIDDLE WAS LIKE THAT. YOU COULD PUT IT ANYWHERE AND YOU KNEW HE'D COME UP WITH IT."

DAN FOUTS, 1988

'74
MEL HEIN

He was the Lou Gehrig of football, the man who played every minute of every New York Giants game for 15 years. One New York writer called Mel Hein "the greatest two-way player in Giants history,"

but he probably was shortsighted in his praise. Hein was the prototype center of the professional game's early years, a trend-setting linebacker and a man who developed football techniques that are still in use today.

formation. Hein, forced to keep his head down longer to ensure accurate delivery, still had the quickness to deliver his block and occasionally even joined sweeps as one of the first pulling linemen.

Legend has it that Hein never made a bad snap, and the techniques he developed have been passed on from center to center for generations. As a mobile 225-pound linebacker, he excelled at pass coverage and used jamming tactics that nobody had seen before. Hein was strong, tough and a 60-minute guarantee for every game, but his greatest asset was the football intelligence he used to develop and master techniques that were well ahead of his time.

Amiable and modest off the field, Hein joined the Giants as a $150-per-game hopeful after a good college

ALL-TIME BEST PLAYERS
SELECTED BY RON WOLF

1. Sammy Baugh
2. Otto Graham
3. Johnny Unitas
4. Jim Brown
5. Don Hutson
6. Jerry Rice
7. Gino Marchetti
8. Joe Greene
9. Mel Hein
10. Dick Butkus

Hein's first priority was as the "second quarterback" of New York's offense from 1931 to '45. In the era of single-wing formations, every snap was directed to a tailback positioned away from the line, the equivalent of snapping in today's shotgun

career at Washington State and served as Giants captain for 10 years. He helped the team qualify for seven championship games and win two NFL titles and was selected to four Pro Bowls, a postseason event that was not founded until 1939, late in his career.

"I'VE BEEN AROUND THIS LEAGUE A LONG TIME AND I'VE NEVER SEEN A PLAYER WHO MADE FEWER MISTAKES THAN MEL. HE HAS A FEEL FOR FOOTBALL, AN INSTINCTIVE UNDERSTANDING AND GRASP OF IT THAT ALLOWS HIM TO COMMAND EVERY BIT OF ACTION ON THE FIELD."

GIANTS COACH STEVE OWEN,
1942, THE SPORTING NEWS

75

MIKE WEBSTER

At first glance, Mike Webster looked like a character out of a Popeye cartoon. His squat, compact body and round, weather-beaten face were accentuated by bulging muscles that seemed to roll out of his short, tight uniform sleeves. But there was nothing funny about the man behind the muscle. He helped power the Pittsburgh Steelers to four Super Bowl wins over a six-year span and spent 17 NFL seasons carving out a legitimate claim as the best center to ever play the game.

Webster's strength was almost legendary, as was the incredible workout regimen he maintained. "He works out at home, comes here for practice and a workout, then goes home to work out again," former Steelers assistant conditioning coach Walt Evans said in 1984. Webster displayed that kind of dedication throughout a career that stretched from 1974 to 1990 and included a consecutive-games streak of 177 and a six-year run in which he didn't miss a play.

The 6-1, 255-pound Webster played with an old-school, no-nonsense, John Wayne-like mentality that allowed him to overcome minor injuries and dominate bigger nose tackles game after game. Some of his success could be traced to the remarkable strength, some to the textbook blocking technique he spent long hours developing. Iron Mike also possessed a field awareness and football savvy that made him the undisputed leader and centerpiece of the Steelers' outstanding offensive line.

MOST INTENSE PLAYERS

SELECTED BY DWIGHT STEPHENSON

1. Dan Marino
2. John Hannah
3. Barry Sanders
4. Andre Tippett
5. Mike Singletary
6. Mike Webster
7. Jackie Slater
8. Tim Krumrie
9. Dan Hampton
10. Ed Newman

Webster, who was born in Tomahawk, Wis., and played at the University of Wisconsin, competed in nine Pro Bowls. He finished his Hall of Fame career with Kansas City in 1989 and 1990 after setting Pittsburgh team records for seasons (15) and games (220).

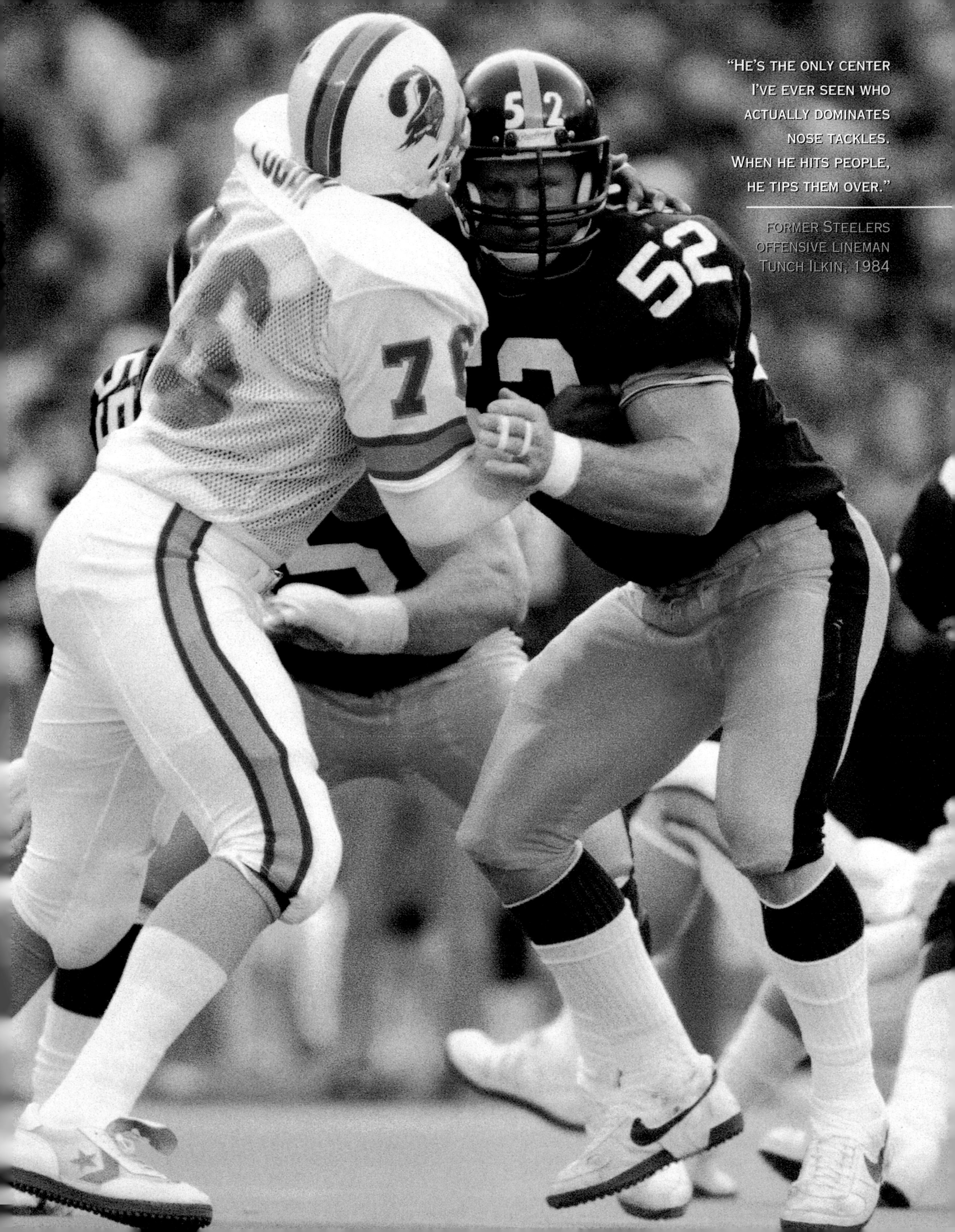

"He's the only center I've ever seen who actually dominates nose tackles. When he hits people, he tips them over."

Former Steelers offensive lineman Tunch Ilkin, 1984

ALL-FRANCHISE TEAMS

The following all-time teams were selected for franchises that have won three or more championships: AFL, NFL or Super Bowl. The choices were made by editors from *The Sporting News*.

BALTIMORE/INDIANAPOLIS COLTS

OFFENSE	DEFENSE
QB—Johnny Unitas	E—Gino Marchetti
RB—Alan Ameche	E—Bubba Smith
RB—Lydell Mitchell	T—Art Donovan
WR—Raymond Berry	T—Big Daddy Lipscomb
WR—Lenny Moore	LB—Mike Curtis
TE—John Mackey	LB—Ted Hendricks
T—Chris Hinton	LB—Don Shinnick
T—Bob Vogel	CB—Bobby Boyd
G—Jim Parker	CB—Eugene Daniel
G—Art Spinney	S—Jerry Logan
C—Ray Donaldson	S—Rich Volk

K—Dean Biasucci; P—Rohn Stark
Coach: Weeb Ewbank

CHICAGO BEARS

OFFENSE	DEFENSE
QB—Sid Luckman	E—Doug Atkins
RB—Walter Payton	E—Richard Dent
RB—Bronko Nagurski/	T—Dan Hampton
Gale Sayers	T—Link Lyman
WR—Harlon Hill	LB—Bill George
WR—Ken Kavanaugh	LB—Dick Butkus
TE—Mike Ditka	LB—Mike Singletary
T—Joe Stydahar	DB—George McAfee
T—George Musso	DB—Richie Petitbon
G—Danny Fortmann	DB—Gary Fencik
G—Stan Jones	DB—Dave Duerson
C—Bulldog Turner	

K—Kevin Butler; P—Bobby Joe Green
Coach: George Halas

CLEVELAND BROWNS

OFFENSE	DEFENSE
QB—Otto Graham	E—Len Ford
RB—Jim Brown	E—Paul Wiggin
RB—Marion Motley	T—Jerry Sherk
WR—Paul Warfield	T—Michael Dean Perry
WR—Dante Lavelli	LB—Clay Matthews
TE—Ozzie Newsome	LB—Chip Banks
T—Mike McCormack	LB—Bill Willis
T—Dick Schafrath	CB—Frank Minnifield
G—Gene Hickerson	CB—Tommy James
G—John Wooten	S—Warren Lahr
C—Frank Gatski	S—Clarence Scott

K—Lou Groza; P—Horace Gillom
Coach: Paul Brown

DALLAS COWBOYS

OFFENSE	DEFENSE
QB—Roger Staubach	E—Ed (Too Tall) Jones
RB—Tony Dorsett	E—Harvey Martin
RB—Emmitt Smith	T—Bob Lilly
WR—Drew Pearson	T—Randy White
WR—Michael Irvin	LB—Lee Roy Jordan
TE—Jay Novacek	LB—Chuck Howley
T—Rayfield Wright	LB—Bob Breunig
T—Ralph Neely	CB—Mel Renfro
G—John Niland	CB—Deion Sanders
G—Larry Allen	S—Cliff Harris
C—Mark Stepnoski	S—Cornell Green

K—Rafael Septien; P—Danny White
Coach: Tom Landry

DETROIT LIONS

OFFENSE	DEFENSE
QB—Bobby Layne	E—Al (Bubba) Baker
RB—Barry Sanders	E—Darris McCord
RB—Billy Sims	T—Doug English
WR—Herman Moore	T—Alex Karras
WR—Gail Cogdill	LB—Joe Schmidt
TE—Charlie Sanders	LB—Wayne Walker
T—Lou Creekmur	LB—Chris Spielman
T—Lomas Brown	CB—Lem Barney
G—Harley Sewell	CB—Dick LeBeau
G—John Gordy	S—Jack Christiansen
C—Alex Wojciechowicz	S—Yale Lary

K—Eddie Murray; P—Yale Lary
Coach: Buddy Parker

GREEN BAY PACKERS

OFFENSE	DEFENSE
QB—Bart Starr	E—Willie Davis
RB—Jim Taylor	E—Reggie White
RB—Paul Hornung	T—Henry Jordan
WR—Don Hutson	T—Dave Hanner
WR—Sterling Sharpe	LB—Ray Nitschke
TE—Ron Kramer	LB—Dave Robinson
T—Forrest Gregg	LB—Bill Forester
T—Cal Hubbard	CB—Herb Adderley
G—Jerry Kramer	CB—Willie Buchanon
G—Fuzzy Thurston	S—Willie Wood
C—Jim Ringo	S—LeRoy Butler

K—Chris Jacke; P—Craig Hentrich
Coach: Vince Lombardi

New York Giants

OFFENSE	DEFENSE
QB—Phil Simms	E—Leonard Marshall
RB—Frank Gifford	E—Andy Robustelli
RB—Rodney Hampton	T—Rosey Grier
WR—Red Badgro	T—Steve Owen
WR—Del Shofner	LB—Sam Huff
TE—Mark Bavaro	LB—Harry Carson
T—Roosevelt Brown	LB—Lawrence Taylor
T—Jumbo Elliott	CB—Mark Haynes
G—Jack Stroud	CB—Dick Lynch
G—Darrell Dess	S—Emlen Tunnell
C—Mel Hein	S—Jim Patton

K—Pete Gogolak; P—Dave Jennings
Coach: Steve Owen

Oakland/L.A. Raiders

OFFENSE	DEFENSE
QB—Ken Stabler	E—Howie Long
RB—Marcus Allen	E—Ben Davidson
RB—Mark van Eeghen	T—Chester McGlockton
WR—Fred Biletnikoff	T—Otis Sistrunk
WR—Tim Brown	LB—Ted Hendricks
TE—Dave Casper	LB—Phil Villapiano
T—Art Shell	LB—Rod Martin
T—Henry Lawrence	CB—Willie Brown
G—Gene Upshaw	CB—Mike Haynes
G—Steve Wisniewski	S—Jack Tatum
C—Jim Otto	S—Vann McElroy

K—George Blanda; P—Ray Guy
Coach: John Madden

Philadelphia Eagles

OFFENSE	DEFENSE
QB—Tommy Thompson	E—Reggie White
RB—Steve Van Buren	E—Clyde Simmons
RB—Wilbert Montgomery	T—Jerome Brown
WR—Tommy McDonald	T—Floyd Peters
WR—Pete Pihos	LB—Chuck Bednarik
TE—Keith Jackson	LB—Bill Bergey
T—Jerry Sisemore	LB—Maxie Baughan
T—Al Wistert	CB—Eric Allen
G—Bucko Kilroy	CB—Roynell Young
G—Ron Baker	S—Bill Bradley
C—Alex Wojciechowicz	S—Tom Brookshier

K—Bobby Walston; P—Joe Muha
Coach: Greasy Neale

Pittsburgh Steelers

OFFENSE	DEFENSE
QB—Terry Bradshaw	E—L.C. Greenwood
RB—Franco Harris	E—Dwight White
RB—John Henry Johnson	T—Joe Greene
WR—John Stallworth	T—Ernie Stautner
WR—Lynn Swann	LB—Jack Ham
TE—Bennie Cunningham	LB—Jack Lambert
T—Tunch Ilkin	LB—Andy Russell
T—Frank Varrichione	CB—Mel Blount
G—Gerry Mullins	CB—Rod Woodson
G—Bruce Van Dyke	S—Donnie Shell
C—Mike Webster	S—Carnell Lake

K—Gary Anderson; P—Bobby Walden
Coach: Chuck Noll

San Francisco 49ers

OFFENSE	DEFENSE
QB—Joe Montana	E—Tommy Hart
RB—Joe Perry	E—Cedrick Hardman
RB—Roger Craig	T—Leo Nomellini
WR—Jerry Rice	T—Charlie Krueger
WR—Billy Wilson	LB—Keena Turner
TE—Brent Jones	LB—Dave Wilcox
T—Bob St. Clair	LB—Charles Haley
T—Keith Fahnhorst	CB—Abe Woodson
G—Guy McIntyre	CB—Jimmy Johnson
G—Randy Cross	S—Ronnie Lott
C—Forrest Blue	S—Merton Hanks

K—Ray Wersching; P—Tommy Davis
Coach: Bill Walsh

Washington Redskins

OFFENSE	DEFENSE
QB—Sammy Baugh	E—Gene Brito
RB—John Riggins	E—Charles Mann
RB—Cliff Battles	T—Dave Butz
WR—Art Monk	T—Diron Talbert
WR—Charley Taylor	LB—Chris Hanburger
TE—Jerry Smith	LB—Ken Harvey
T—Joe Jacoby	LB—Chuck Drazenovich
T—Turk Edwards	CB—Darrell Green
G—Russ Grimm	CB—Pat Fischer
G—Vince Promuto	S—Ken Houston
C—Len Hauss	S—Brig Owens

K—Mark Moseley; P—Sammy Baugh
Coach: Joe Gibbs

"IT'S UNCANNY THE WAY HUFF FOLLOWS THE BALL.
HE IGNORES ALL THE THINGS YOU DO TO GET HIM AWAY
FROM THE PLAY AND HE COMES AFTER THE BALL
WHEREVER IT'S THROWN OR WHEREVER THE RUN GOES.
HE SEEMS TO BE ALL OVER THE FIELD AT ONCE."

VINCE LOMBARDI

76 SAM HUFF

uff, Huff, Huff. Huff, Huff, Huff." The cheer chugged around Yankee Stadium like a giant steam engine, much the way New York Giants middle linebacker Sam Huff chugged around the field on his typical Sunday afternoon search-and-destroy mission. It was a Big Apple love affair, big No. 70 and a city that appreciated its heroes. When Huff delivered another crunching blow, everybody celebrated.

There was a lot to like about the 6-1, 230-pound Huff, who charmed fans with his warm, engaging personality and dismantled game plans with punishing regularity. Huff was not the fastest or strongest linebacker in the league, but he more than made up for shortcomings with hard work, dedication, uncanny anticipation and the ability to diagnose plays. He always seemed to be around the ball, whether blitzing, stuffing a run or making one of his 30 career interceptions.

And he always seemed to be in the spotlight. Huff, using the New York media stage to glamorize the linebacker position, became the first defensive player to gain national attention. He was featured on the cover of *Time* at age 24 and in a CBS television documentary called "The Violent World of Sam Huff" a few years later. His fame was enhanced by the success of the Giants, who captured one championship and appeared in six title games in his eight New York seasons (1956-63).

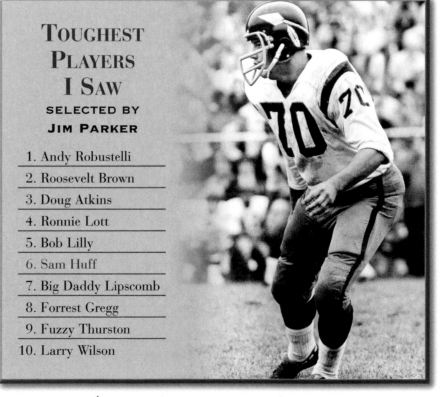

TOUGHEST PLAYERS I SAW

SELECTED BY JIM PARKER

1. Andy Robustelli
2. Roosevelt Brown
3. Doug Atkins
4. Ronnie Lott
5. Bob Lilly
6. Sam Huff
7. Big Daddy Lipscomb
8. Forrest Gregg
9. Fuzzy Thurston
10. Larry Wilson

The enthusiastic and unflinchingly loyal Huff, who is remembered for his classic and bruising battles against Cleveland's Jim Brown and Green Bay's Jim Taylor, was stunned when his beloved Giants announced a 1964 trade that sent him to Washington, where he played another five successful seasons. A five-time Pro Bowl choice, Huff was bitter toward the Giants but continued to smile and attack ballcarriers with a fury that lasted until 1969, when he retired as a player/coach under Vince Lombardi.

77 STEVE VAN BUREN

"THORPE WAS A BIGGER MAN
THAN VAN BUREN,
OUTWEIGHED HIM BY 10
POUNDS AND WAS
TWO INCHES TALLER.
YET STEVE DOES THE SAME
THINGS AS THORPE.
THERE IS ONE DIFFERENCE.
WHEN THORPE HIT, HE DID
SO WITH HIS KNEES. STEVE
USES THE SHOULDER—
AND WITH TERRIFIC POWER."

EAGLES LINE COACH
JOHN KELLISON, 1948
THE SPORTING NEWS

He was easy to spot. Broad shoulders, a strong upper body, a slim, tapered waist and powerful legs supported a 6-foot, 200-pound frame, making Steve Van Buren stand out in any crowd. He was especially noticeable when he tucked a football under his right arm, the signal to defensive players throughout the NFL that the "Movin' Van" was getting ready to rumble.

Van Buren, simply stated, was the best running back of the 1940s, a worthy successor to the Jim Thorpe/Bronko Nagurski power-running style and the predecessor to coming stars Marion Motley, Jim Brown and Jim Taylor. Van Buren was a no-nonsense, up-the-middle runner with enough speed to make a cut on unsuspecting defenders and enough power to run over them.

Van Buren, who was born in Honduras and raised in New Orleans, approached his craft with a shy, country kid modesty, even after a spectacular senior season at LSU in which he led the country in rushing. Philadelphia Eagles coach Earle "Greasy" Neale, recognizing the steamroller power, agility and speed combination Van Buren brought to the field, designed an offense around him and watched his Eagles win three straight division titles and consecutive championships in 1948 and 1949.

Neale also watched Van Buren win four rushing and scoring titles in a record-setting career. He set a season mark in 1947 with 1,008 yards and raised the bar to 1,146 two years later. When he retired after the 1951 season with a record 5,860 yards, he also held marks for rushing attempts, rushing touchdowns, most touchdowns in a season, most years leading the league in rushing and most rushing yards in a title game (196 in a 1949 victory over the Los Angeles Rams). The versatile Van Buren also was an accomplished return man and capable receiver.

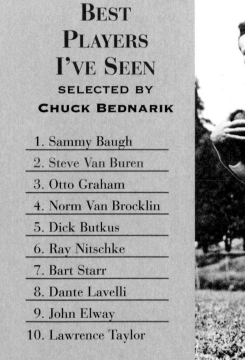

BEST PLAYERS I'VE SEEN

SELECTED BY
CHUCK BEDNARIK

1. Sammy Baugh
2. Steve Van Buren
3. Otto Graham
4. Norm Van Brocklin
5. Dick Butkus
6. Ray Nitschke
7. Bart Starr
8. Dante Lavelli
9. John Elway
10. Lawrence Taylor

78

JIM OTTO

"REMEMBER THOSE MOVIES IN WHICH A GUY WALKS IN
WITH HIS FOOTBALL SHOES DRAPED OVER HIS SHOULDER?
HE SPITS ON HIS HANDS, RUBS DIRT IN HIS PALMS AND
SAYS, 'LET'S GO.' WELL, THAT'S JIM OTTO."

JOHN MADDEN, 1975
THE SPORTING NEWS

He was a charter member of the American Football League, an Oakland Raiders original and the only All-AFL center in the league's 10-year existence. Nobody exhibited more domination of a position over a 15-year stretch than Jim Otto. Despite 10 broken noses and numerous knee operations, Otto always made it on the field, starting in all 210 of his team's regular-season games and 13 postseason contests over 15 years.

Life could have been a lot different for Otto.

Undrafted by the NFL after his college career at Miami (Fla.), he was a late-round AFL pick who showed up in 1960 at the Raiders' first camp weighing an unimpressive 205 pounds. But he quickly showed the heart and determination that would propel him to all-star status. By 1961, he had beefed up his 6-2 frame to 255 pounds and attracted attention with overpowering performances against bigger nose tackles and faster linebackers.

Otto, whose star recognition was enhanced by the two big zeroes he wore on his uniform jersey, was an outgoing, easy-to-like charmer whose oversized head (size 8½ helmet) was covered by platinum blond hair. But on the field, he was an old-school competitor who used superior speed and techniques to range well beyond the usual blocking assignments for centers. Described by one opponent as "meaner than a bear and tougher than an old boot," Otto was the leader and signal-caller for an outstanding line that was fortified in the late 1960s by fellow Hall of Famers Art Shell and Gene Upshaw.

Otto's pride and leadership were instrumental in the Raiders' transformation from an AFL doormat into one of pro football's most successful franchises. With him in the middle, they won seven division titles and one AFL championship, losing to Green Bay in Super Bowl II. He also was selected to 12 Pro Bowls.

LONGEST TENURED AFL PLAYERS

Rk. Name	AFL Seasons	Rk. Name	AFL Seasons
1. George Blanda	10	7. Bobby Bell	7
Don Maynard	10	Willie Brown	7
Ron Mix	10	Buck Buchanan	7
Jim Otto	10	10. Fred Biletnikoff	5
5. Lance Alworth	8	Joe Namath	5
Lenny Dawson	8		

"HE BECAME A PART OF THE
REAL IDENTITY OF OUR TEAM,
THE GOOD, TOUGH RUNNING
GAME. AS TIME WENT ON, HE
WAS A REAL INSPIRATION FOR
US, NOT JUST THE WAY HE
ALWAYS PLAYED BUT ALSO
FOR HIS INFLUENCE ON OUR
YOUNGER PLAYERS."

FORMER DOLPHINS COACH
DON SHULA

79

LARRY LITTLE

They called him a sledgehammer, the path-clearing enforcer for Miami's power running attack in the 1970s. Larry Little was the antithesis of his name, a 6-1, 265-pound guard who could outfinesse defensive tackles and overwhelm cornerbacks like a runaway truck. He was the point man for a talented unit that triggered three straight Super Bowl appearances and the hatchet man who helped make household names of Larry Csonka, Jim Kiick and Mercury Morris.

Little was fast and quick, a lesson learned by defenders he was assigned to block and unfortunate linebackers and defensive backs who had to deal with him on power sweeps. That's when he was at his intimidating best, pulling to his right and attacking with full-speed ferocity anyone who dared challenge the runner. Little was a rumbling wide body who considered every play, every block a matter of respect.

That was a product of the diminutive $750 free-agent bonus Little got from San Diego in 1967 after a college career at Bethune-Cookman. Chargers coach Sid Gillman experimented with the 285-pounder at several positions, including fullback, before dealing him to the Dolphins in 1969. It didn't take long for coach Don Shula to get Little down to 265 and make him the durable centerpiece for a line that would clear the way for 2,000-yard rushing seasons every year in the '70s.

The gregarious, confident Little was a 10-year captain and inspirational role model for younger players. He also was visible in the community, where his charity work became almost as legendary as his crushing blocks. A five-time Pro Bowl selection who retired after the 1980 season, Little was a force for

PLAYERS OVERLOOKED IN NFL DRAFT

(THE FOLLOWING TOP 100 PLAYERS WERE EITHER UNDRAFTED OR LOW PICKS BY NFL TEAMS)

Name	Rd./FA	Year
Raymond Berry	20	1954
George Blanda	12	1949
Roosevelt Brown	27	1953
Willie Brown	FA	1963
Willie Davis	15	1956
Deacon Jones	14	1961
Night Train Lane	FA	1952
Larry Little	FA	1967
Bart Starr	17	1956
Emlen Tunnell	FA	1948

powerful 1971, '72 and '73 Dolphins teams that lost one Super Bowl and won two. The 1972 team ran for 2,960 yards and recorded the first undefeated and untied season (including playoffs) in NFL history and the 1973 team finished with 2,521 rushing yards and a 15-2 record.

"HE IS THREE OR FOUR MEN ROLLED INTO ONE. HE IS JACK DEMPSEY, BABE RUTH, AL JOLSON, PAAVO NURMI AND MAN O' WAR."

DAMON RUNYON

80

RED GRANGE

He was an honest-to-God hero, a bigger-than-life superstar in the class of 1920s contemporaries Babe Ruth, Jack Dempsey, Bill Tilden and Bobby Jones. Red Grange was the Galloping Ghost from the University of Illinois, the legend upon which the NFL was constructed. When No. 77 ran with the football, fans flocked to watch, the media took notice and professional football was the center of the sports universe.

Grange's contributions should be measured in status and fan appeal rather than yardage or years.

Today's professional game took root when Grange signed an incredible share-the-gate contract with the Chicago Bears after his final 1925 college game and played an exhibition before a packed house of 36,000 at Wrigley Field. Hundreds of thousands would stream through the turnstiles over the next few months during a wild season-ending and exhibition-game tour that featured eight games in one 11-day stretch.

What they saw was the effortless glide, ghostlike weave, explosive speed and nimble elusiveness that had carried Grange to legendary fame at Illinois. He was equally dangerous on running plays or kick returns and Bears coach George Halas conceived the man-in-motion maneuver to free him for pass receptions. Grange's willingness to block and his humble manner made him popular among both teammates and opponents, who appreciated his trailblazing efforts.

The whirlwind 1925 exhibition tour brought Grange fortune, but it also wore him down. After a wasted 1926 season in which the 180-pound Grange was the central figure for an ill-fated rival league, he returned to the NFL with the New York Yankees and suffered a knee injury that kept him on the sideline through 1928. He returned to the Bears from 1929 through 1934, but the knee, protected by a brace, limited him to mere mortal status.

SKILL-POSITION HALL OF FAMERS COACHED BY GEORGE HALAS

Name	Pos.	Name	Pos.
Paddy Driscoll	RB	George McAfee	RB/DB
Red Grange	RB/DB	Bobby Layne	QB
Bronko Nagurski	FB/DT	George Blanda	QB/K
Bill Hewitt	E	Mike Ditka	TE
Sid Luckman	QB/DB	Gale Sayers	RB

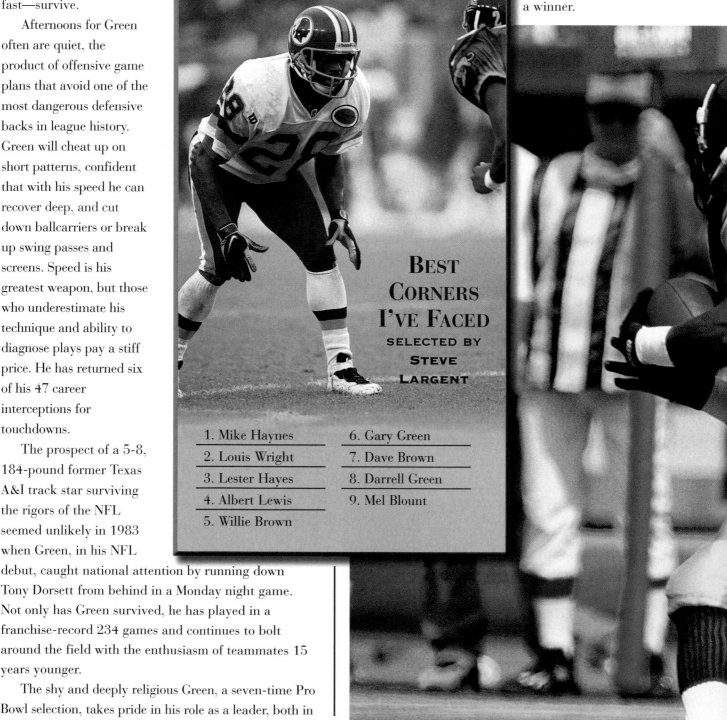

He arrived as the fastest man in the NFL and he might depart the same way—more than a decade and a half later. The step Darrell Green reportedly has lost over 16 seasons with the Washington Redskins might be nothing more than a rumor, a psychological ploy to give the league's top receivers a fighting chance. At age 39, he remains one of the league's most-efficient cover cornerbacks, an uncompromising role at which only the strong—and fast—survive.

Afternoons for Green often are quiet, the product of offensive game plans that avoid one of the most dangerous defensive backs in league history. Green will cheat up on short patterns, confident that with his speed he can recover deep, and cut down ballcarriers or break up swing passes and screens. Speed is his greatest weapon, but those who underestimate his technique and ability to diagnose plays pay a stiff price. He has returned six of his 47 career interceptions for touchdowns.

The prospect of a 5-8, 184-pound former Texas A&I track star surviving the rigors of the NFL seemed unlikely in 1983 when Green, in his NFL debut, caught national attention by running down Tony Dorsett from behind in a Monday night game. Not only has Green survived, he has played in a franchise-record 234 games and continues to bolt around the field with the enthusiasm of teammates 15 years younger.

The shy and deeply religious Green, a seven-time Pro Bowl selection, takes pride in his role as a leader, both in the locker room and the community. Teammates are constantly amazed by the quality of play and passion he brings to every game at a career stage when most aging corners have been either moved to safety or exiled into retirement. That passion is reflected by his three Super Bowl appearances—two as a winner.

BEST CORNERS I'VE FACED

SELECTED BY STEVE LARGENT

1. Mike Haynes	6. Gary Green
2. Louis Wright	7. Dave Brown
3. Lester Hayes	8. Darrell Green
4. Albert Lewis	9. Mel Blount
5. Willie Brown	

81 DARRELL GREEN

"I'VE BEEN WATCHING HIM
SINCE I WAS REAL SMALL.
HE CAN DO ANYTHING,
REALLY. HE'S REAL FAST
AND HE CAN JUMP
TO THE SKY."

CHAMP BAILEY, 1999

82

BRETT FAVRE

He arrived with a warning: has exceptional physical skills but a reckless, gunslinger style that can be hazardous to an offense. Seven years later, Brett Favre is living proof that swashbuckling quarterbacks still can thrive in the NFL, where the virtues of patience, control and discipline are preached and practiced on Sunday afternoons. He's a throwback, an unpredictable sniper who has produced big plays, points and victories while leading a once-proud franchise back to Super Bowl prominence.

Favre has what scouts call an explosive arm, a weapon he deploys often as the general of Green Bay's West Coast offense. Opposing coaches call him scary, a tribute to his ability to throw short or deep, on the run or from the pocket, and to improvise and make positive things happen when all else fails. Favre is especially dangerous in the red zone, where he frequently goes for broke and wings defense-deflating touchdown passes into the smallest of openings.

The numbers certainly are scary: two 4,000-yard passing seasons, five 3,000-yarders, an NFL-record five straight seasons with 30 or more touchdown passes, an 89.0 career passer rating, a .617 completion percentage and five Pro Bowl selections. Favre's gambles sometimes result in interceptions, but his decision-making abilities have consistently improved

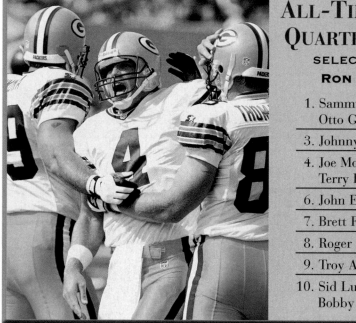

ALL-TIME BEST QUARTERBACKS
SELECTED BY RON WOLF

1. Sammy Baugh
   Otto Graham
3. Johnny Unitas
4. Joe Montana
   Terry Bradshaw
6. John Elway
7. Brett Favre
8. Roger Staubach
9. Troy Aikman
10. Sid Luckman
    Bobby Layne

and he enters 1999 with 109 consecutive starts.

Favre's flamboyant style is an extension of his carefree personality. Teammates describe him as a big, fun-loving kid without the ego that usually goes with postseason success. Favre's powerful arm carried the Packers to the NFC championship game after the 1995 season and to the Super Bowl a year later, ending three decades of Green Bay frustration. The Packers won that game against New England, thanks to Favre's 54- and 81-yard touchdown passes, and returned to the Super Bowl spotlight a year later, only to lose to Denver.

"I THINK WHEN BRETT GOES THROUGH HIS FIRST TWO OPTIONS AND THEN HAS TO IMPROVISE, THAT IS WHEN THE PLAY REALLY STARTS. HE JUST KEEPS MAKING PLAYS AND BREAKING YOUR HEART."

BUCCANEERS SAFETY JOHN LYNCH, 1998
TSN PRO FOOTBALL YEARBOOK

83
FRANCO HARRIS

H e was a small, quick man trapped in a large body, an almost perfect blend of power and finesse. Franco Harris spent 13 NFL seasons trapped between mandates to drive his 230 pounds through tacklers and a personal preference to go around them. Career totals of 12,120 yards and 91 rushing touchdowns suggest he found a happy median, as do the four Super Bowl rings he earned as chief grinder for Pittsburgh's winning machine of the 1970s.

Harris was a quiet, serious, painfully slow-moving personality who shifted into a faster, more-competitive mode when he pulled the Steelers' black helmet over his dark, bearded face. The body suggested power, but Harris had great balance, quick change-of-direction moves and explosive speed. Critics questioned his dancing-for-daylight style and unwillingness to fight for extra yards, but Harris claimed that his avoid-unnecessary-contact mentality extended his career.

Harris did not punish like Earl Campbell and he wasn't flashy like Tony Dorsett. He was more like a marathon runner who always reached the finish line. Eight times he topped 1,000 yards in a season, 47 times he topped 100 in a game; he remains the all-time leader in postseason (1,556) and Super Bowl (354) rushing yards. Harris, a nine-time Pro Bowl selection, was especially good when it counted, the man who would get key yards in critical situations.

He also was versatile enough to catch 307 passes over 13 seasons (12 with Pittsburgh, one with Seattle), and will be remembered for the "Immaculate Reception" he made to defeat the Oakland Raiders in a 1972 first-round playoff game—the first postseason win in Pittsburgh history. It was a fitting culmination to a

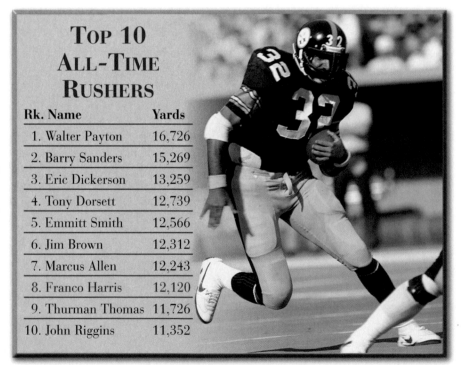

Rk.	Name	Yards
1.	Walter Payton	16,726
2.	Barry Sanders	15,269
3.	Eric Dickerson	13,259
4.	Tony Dorsett	12,739
5.	Emmitt Smith	12,566
6.	Jim Brown	12,312
7.	Marcus Allen	12,243
8.	Franco Harris	12,120
9.	Thurman Thomas	11,726
10.	John Riggins	11,352

TOP 10 ALL-TIME RUSHERS

storybook 1,055-yard rookie season that inspired formation of "Franco's Italian Army," a Steelers rooting section. When he retired in 1984, Harris ranked third on football's all-time rushing charts, behind Jim Brown and Walter Payton.

84

DWIGHT STEPHENSON

"MAN, I'VE NEVER SEEN ANYONE LIKE HIM. I JUST DON'T KNOW HOW HE DOES IT, HOW HE CAN SNAP THE BALL WITH ONE HAND AND BE OFF EXPLODING INTO HIS BLOCK ALL IN ONE MOTION."

FORMER DOLPHINS DEFENSIVE LINEMAN MIKE CHARLES, 1985

A labama's Bear Bryant once called him "the greatest center I've ever coached." So did Miami's Don Shula. Teammates and opponents marveled at the unrelenting ferocity he unleashed after every snap of his massive wrists. Dwight Stephenson was a human destroyer, a protector of quarterback Dan Marino and the perfect middle man for one of the better offensive lines of the 1980s.

The finely chiseled Stephenson was like an angry panther when he snapped the ball and exploded his 255-pound body into a defender. He was strong, fast and devoted to the challenge of becoming the best center in NFL history. Stephenson operated at a special level of intensity and the Dolphins constructed their blocking schemes around his ability to handle nose tackles and linebackers one-on-one. Trying to get past Stephenson was like trying to wrestle a bear.

Run-blocking or pass-blocking, Stephenson was equally proficient. He was a tireless worker who approached every practice as if it were the Super Bowl and worked out during offseasons as if his life depended on it. Coaches marveled at his play every time they broke down game film, and he once went two seasons without allowing a sack.

Tenacious as Stephenson was on the field, he was gentle and friendly off it. A deeply religious man with a charming smile, he winced every time teammates talked up his sometimes-amazing feats. Like the time he took out two rushers at the same time, one with each forearm. Or the time he blocked a defender out of the end zone. A five-time Pro Bowl selection in his eight seasons, Stephenson saw his career come to a premature end in 1987 when a defender hit him on the knee, tearing the anterior cruciate ligament.

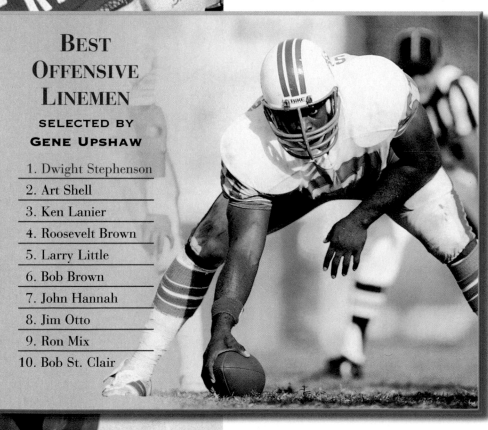

BEST OFFENSIVE LINEMEN

SELECTED BY
GENE UPSHAW

1. Dwight Stephenson
2. Art Shell
3. Ken Lanier
4. Roosevelt Brown
5. Larry Little
6. Bob Brown
7. John Hannah
8. Jim Otto
9. Ron Mix
10. Bob St. Clair

"CHARLEY WAS ONE OF THE FINEST ALL-AROUND RECEIVERS—SIZE, SPEED AND AGILITY. BUT WHAT I REMEMBER MOST ABOUT HIM WAS HIS ABILITY TO BLOCK DOWNFIELD. HE WAS A VERY COMPLETE WIDE RECEIVER. A VERY BIG AND COMPLETE WIDE RECEIVER."

LEM BARNEY, 1999

85

CHARLEY TAYLOR

N ew York Giants scout Emlen Tunnell called Washington rookie Charley Taylor "the best back to come into the NFL since Ollie Matson and Hugh McElhenny." Taylor envisioned himself as the

next Jim Brown. But Redskins coach Otto Graham looked past the obvious athletic ability, the natural instincts and the explosive breakaway speed to spot a wide receiver in running back's clothing, a big-play machine that would dissect opposing secondaries for 13 seasons.

Graham's wise 1966 switch was fought bitterly by Taylor, who had run for 755 yards and caught 53 passes for 814 more in an outstanding 1964 rookie season. But it didn't take long to see that the 6-3, 210-pound Taylor, isolated against smaller defensive backs and catching passes from Sonny Jurgensen, was a big play waiting to happen. The speed and quickness that got him to the holes ahead of his blockers as a runner became a devastating weapon on pass routes and runs after receptions.

The former Arizona State star blossomed quickly, catching league-leading totals of 72 and 70 passes in 1966 and '67—two of the seven seasons he would top the 50 plateau. He became an outstanding technician who could go short or long with sure hands and the ability to improvise when a play

broke down. But he took most pride in his all-around game, which he punctuated with fierce downfield and crackback blocks.

Taylor's always-positive attitude and popularity earned him a captain's stripe under coach George Allen

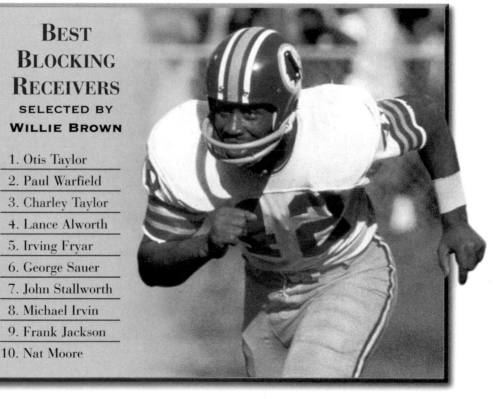

BEST BLOCKING RECEIVERS
SELECTED BY
WILLIE BROWN

1. Otis Taylor
2. Paul Warfield
3. Charley Taylor
4. Lance Alworth
5. Irving Fryar
6. George Sauer
7. John Stallworth
8. Michael Irvin
9. Frank Jackson
10. Nat Moore

before he retired in 1977 with a then-record 649 catches, good for 9,110 yards. An eight-time Pro Bowl selection, Taylor scored 90 touchdowns, 79 through the air, and appeared in one Super Bowl (a loss to Miami after the 1972 season).

86

JACK CHRISTIANSEN

The calm, clean, crew-cut look and disarming smile masked a Mr. Hyde scowl that unnerved receivers and quarterbacks when he stepped on the field. Jack Christiansen, defensive back, was nobody's Mr. Nice Guy, especially when his pride was at stake. He was fearless, mean and sneaky, not above throwing a little dirt in a pass catcher's eyes or resorting to any trick that might help his Detroit Lions win a game.

The lanky Christiansen (6-1, 185) was one of the first players drafted to play strictly defense. Lions coach Buddy Parker grabbed him out of Colorado A&M (Colorado State) in 1951 and gave him freedom to roam, practically inventing the position of free safety. Athletic, quick to the ball and blessed with explosive speed, Christiansen had an uncanny ability to look through the receiver, anticipate the quarterback's throw and swoop to the ball.

It didn't take long for him to show another talent as well. In his rookie season, Christiansen returned four punts for touchdowns, two in games against Los Angeles and Green Bay. Former Cleveland star Mac Speedie said the Browns operated by two basic rules when they played the Lions: "Don't throw in his area and don't kick to him on punts." When the long-striding, quick-cutting Christiansen got to full speed, few could catch him. The spread punt formation was invented to defend against his returns.

Detroit's defense, known affectionately as Chris' Crew, became the scourge of the NFL and keyed the Lions' run to championships in 1952, '53 and '57. He teamed in the backfield with fellow Hall of Famer Yale Lary and brought awareness to the secondary. Christiansen retired after the 1958 season with 46 interceptions and averages of 12.8 yards per punt return and 22.5 per kickoff return. Eight of his 13 career TDs came on punt returns.

ALL-TIME PUNT-RETURN AVERAGE
(BASED ON 75 OR MORE RETURNS)

Rk. Name	No.	Avg.
1. Darrien Gordon	177	13.2
2. George McAfee	112	12.8
3. Jack Christiansen	85	12.8
4. Claude Gibson	110	12.6
5. Bill Dudley	124	12.2
6. Rick Upchurch	248	12.1
7. Desmond Howard	164	12.1
8. Billy Johnson	282	11.8
9. Mack Herron	84	11.7
10. Billy Thompson	157	11.6

THE SPORTING NEWS SELECTS FOOTBALL'S 100 GREATEST PLAYERS

"I FIGURE THE DIFFERENCE
BETWEEN OUR 1951 SEASON (7-4-1)
AND 1952 (AN NFL CHAMPIONSHIP)
WAS CHRISTIANSEN. HE WAS
INSTRUMENTAL IN THE OVERALL
DEVELOPMENT OF OUR DEFENSE.
HE RAN IT AND HE WAS THE BOSS.
IT WAS KNOWN AS 'CHRIS' CREW.'"

FORMER LIONS COACH
BUDDY PARKER, 1967

87

ROD WOODSON

"THE BIGGEST THING ABOUT ROD WOODSON,
WHEN THE GAME WAS ON THE LINE
AND YOU WERE FLIRTING WITH HIM,
YOU WERE FLIRTING WITH DANGER.
THAT'S THE BEST WAY TO DESCRIBE HIM.
HE IS A VERY TOUGH GUY. HE IS NOT A GUY
WHO WEARS AN 'S' ON HIS JERSEY
AND STRUTS AROUND, BUT HE IS TOUGH.
YOU DON'T HAVE TO QUESTION WHETHER
YOU WANT HIM IN YOUR FOX HOLE OR NOT."

HALL OF FAME TIGHT END OZZIE NEWSOME

all him a survivor, a cornerback who has lived on the edge for 12 grueling NFL seasons. Rod Woodson has dared to match his aggressive, reckless style against the fastest, smartest wide receivers and has prospered, a marvelous accomplishment in the fast-paced, offensive world of the NFL. He also has thrived as a gifted, big-play performer in a position not always noted for producing difference-makers.

If speed kills, then Woodson should have been outlawed years ago. But there's more to the sculpted 6-0, 200-pound body than fast feet, as the Pittsburgh Steelers discovered in 1987 when they unveiled one of the great coverage corners in football history. The former Purdue star combined a blue-collar work ethic with the athletic skills of a world-class hurdler, a talent he displayed before making football his career.

Woodson has survived because he's fearless and able to block out bad memories, which have been the undoing of many talented corners. As a longtime player in the physical AFC Central, he is an attack man who likes to go nose-to-nose with a receiver, hit him hard and disrupt the timing so prevalent in contemporary passing games. He also can be an overpowering blitzer and seldom makes mistakes on run support.

It's all a byproduct of hard work and pride, which always have been key elements in Woodson's game. The seven-time Pro Bowl selection is thoughtful and contemplative, qualities he passed on as the longtime intellectual leader in the Steelers' locker room before free agency took him to San Francisco in 1997 and Baltimore in '98.

Woodson, who played in Super Bowl XXX with the Steelers after making a remarkable recovery from reconstructive knee surgery, enters the 1999 season with 47 interceptions, including seven that he has returned for touchdowns.

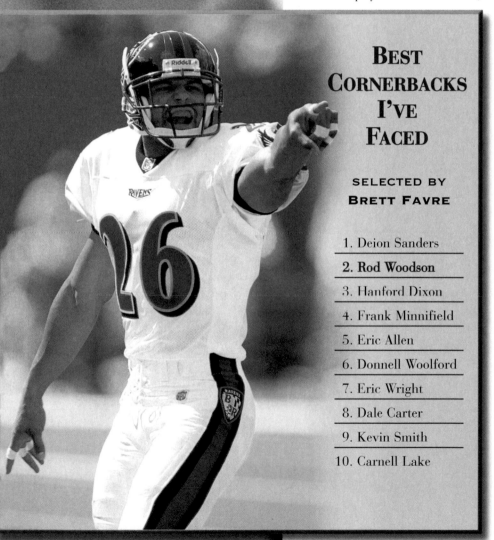

BEST CORNERBACKS I'VE FACED

SELECTED BY BRETT FAVRE

1. Deion Sanders
2. **Rod Woodson**
3. Hanford Dixon
4. Frank Minnifield
5. Eric Allen
6. Donnell Woolford
7. Eric Wright
8. Dale Carter
9. Kevin Smith
10. Carnell Lake

"JIM THORPE COULD HAVE MADE ANY TEAM IN ANY LEAGUE. WHAT'S MORE, HE WOULD HAVE BEEN THE BEST PLAYER ON THAT TEAM. HE WOULD HAVE BEEN THE BEST PLAYER IN THE LEAGUE. THERE WASN'T ANYTHING HE COULDN'T DO BETTER THAN ANYONE ELSE."

HALL OF FAME PLAYER/COACH
JIMMY CONZELMAN, 1963

88

JIM THORPE

H e guards the main entrance to the Pro Football Hall of Fame museum, threatening to deliver one of his dreaded stiff-arms or to trample anyone in his path. The lifesize statue of Jim Thorpe prepares visitors for their nostalgic trip into pro football's past, much as the real Thorpe prepared fans for pro football future eight decades ago. The name and legend are still powerful, and his exploits are recounted with flair and exaggeration. But one thing that cannot be exaggerated is Thorpe's role as the game's first great running back, first gate attraction and spiritual guru.

Thorpe had gained worldwide acclaim as a college football hero for the Carlisle Indian School and a double gold medal winner in the 1912 Olympics before he played his first professional football game in 1915 for the Canton Bulldogs. Thick-armed with a moon face, 42-inch chest and penetrating black eyes, Thorpe was first and foremost a great athlete, maybe the most versatile of the first half century. He complemented his football career by playing major league baseball.

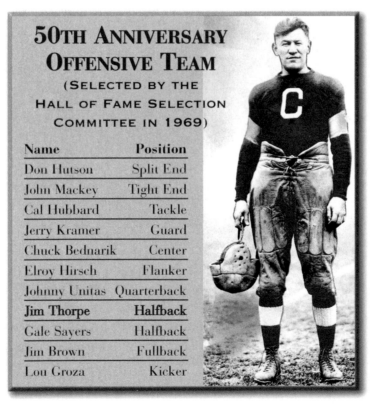

50TH ANNIVERSARY OFFENSIVE TEAM

(SELECTED BY THE HALL OF FAME SELECTION COMMITTEE IN 1969)

Name	Position
Don Hutson	Split End
John Mackey	Tight End
Cal Hubbard	Tackle
Jerry Kramer	Guard
Chuck Bednarik	Center
Elroy Hirsch	Flanker
Johnny Unitas	Quarterback
Jim Thorpe	**Halfback**
Gale Sayers	Halfback
Jim Brown	Fullback
Lou Groza	Kicker

Those who competed against Thorpe remember a high-stepping, stiff-arming muscle man who could run the sweep with outstanding speed, slam down defenders or shed tacklers with an unusual hip twist.

A Native American of Sac and Fox heritage, the 6-1, 190-pound Thorpe also was a gifted passer, a devastating blocker and a kicker who could dominate games with long punts, placements or drop kicks.

The greatness of Thorpe can't be measured by numbers or team accomplishments. After helping Canton to three Ohio League championships before the NFL was formed, he wandered from team to team until 1928, when he retired at age 41. But his most lasting contributions were as the first president of what is now the NFL and as the unparalleled gate attraction who kept the NFL afloat in its formative years.

89

ELROY HIRSCH

"TALK ABOUT THE GENT WHO ZIGGED
WHEN HE SHOULD HAVE ZAGGED.
ROY ALSO HAS A 'ZOG' AND A COUPLE OF
VARIETIES OF 'ZUG' WHEN HE'S UNDER
FULL STEAM."

RAMS QUARTERBACK
NORM VAN BROCKLIN, 1953

Start with those Crazy Legs, the long, muscular limbs that appeared to gyrate in six different directions when shifted into warp speed. Elroy Hirsch walked like a duck but ran pass patterns like an awkward young gazelle trying to evade a hungry pursuer. He was quick, elusive and deceptively fast, a deep-threat receiver who terrorized defensive backs for 12 pro seasons. When Crazy Legs turned on the burners, somebody usually got scorched.

"Spectacular" and "colorful" are words usually associated with Hirsch, who caught 17 touchdown passes in an outstanding 1951 season for the Los Angeles Rams—nine of 44 yards or longer. Hirsch's speed was complemented by near-perfect timing and long, thin fingers that could pull in over-the-head throws while he was in full stride. Once the ball was secured, nobody caught Hirsch from behind.

The nickname was pinned on a 6-2, 190-pound halfback who displayed elusive running skills as well as susceptibility to injury during his college career and three years with the Chicago Rockets of the All-America Football Conference. Hirsch changed positions in 1950, his second season with the Rams, and became one of the first ends to move outside as a flanker. For seven years he teamed with Tom Fears as one of first great receiver tandems.

A blithe spirit who was infectiously happy, intelligent and always ready with a quick quip or putdown, Hirsch helped put the word "bomb" in the NFL dictionary. During his big 1951 season, he averaged 22.7 yards per catch and helped the Rams win a championship, the last in franchise history. His 18.4-yard career average ranks among the best in NFL history and he once caught touchdown passes in 11 straight games (over the 1950 and 1951 seasons), a record since surpassed by Jerry Rice. Hirsch retired in 1957 with 343 catches in nine NFL seasons.

RECEIVERS I MOST ADMIRE

SELECTED BY
RAYMOND BERRY

1. Jerry Rice
2. Elroy Hirsch
3. Steve Largent
4. Lance Alworth
5. Charley Taylor
6. Stanley Morgan
7. Harlon Hill
8. Bob Hayes
9. Harold Jackson
10. Fred Biletnikoff

90

MIKE DITKA

The bristly crew cut topped a chubby face that featured a small mouth, flaring nostrils and narrow, deeply set eyes. If you looked closely at the eyes, you could see the blazing fire that burned within Mike Ditka.

It raged every time he took the field for 12 NFL seasons in a career that redefined the tight end position. And it stoked the imagination of Chicago fans, who embraced him as one of the most popular players in the Bears' long history.

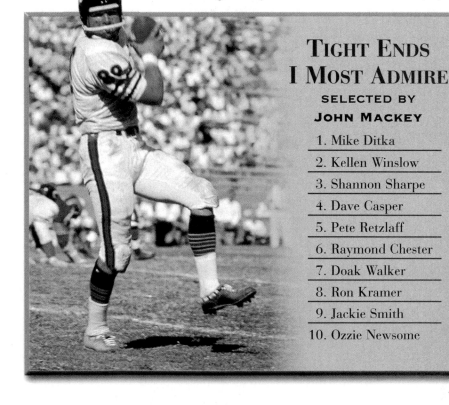

TIGHT ENDS I MOST ADMIRE

SELECTED BY
JOHN MACKEY

1. Mike Ditka
2. Kellen Winslow
3. Shannon Sharpe
4. Dave Casper
5. Pete Retzlaff
6. Raymond Chester
7. Doak Walker
8. Ron Kramer
9. Jackie Smith
10. Ozzie Newsome

much more in mind. Big (6-3, 228 pounds), fast and agile, Ditka became a major weapon, a pass-catching force over the middle and outside who could go long if crowded by a defender.

His rookie season produced amazing numbers—56 catches, 1,076 yards, 12 touchdowns—and sent defensive coordinators scurrying to find a solution. Not only was the bull-necked, broad-shouldered Ditka hard to tackle when he caught the ball, he defiantly stiff-armed his way past tacklers and had the speed to outrun many defensive backs. He consistently flashed his renowned temper and every-play intensity, giving him an intimidating edge over opponents.

Ditka's first four seasons were phenomenal, but the continual pounding took a toll and his pass-catching numbers declined. A trade to Philadelphia was followed by mediocre 1967 and 1968 seasons and another trade to Dallas, where he spent his final four seasons as an outstanding blocker and pass-catching threat for the talented Cowboys. Ditka, a five-time Pro Bowl choice, was a driving force for the Bears' 1963 championship team and he competed in two Super Bowls for Dallas, one a winner over Miami.

Before Ditka was drafted out of Pittsburgh in 1961, tight ends were hard-nosed blockers who occasionally caught a pass over the middle. Iron Mike fit the blocking profile, but Bears coach George Halas had

"MAYBE SOME DAY THERE WILL BE ONE BETTER THAN DITKA. BUT YOU MIGHT SAY THAT MIKE WAS INVENTED TO BE A TIGHT END. HE JUST GOT A GENEROUS HELPING OF EVERYTHING YOU NEED."

FORMER EAGLES
RECEIVER
PETE RETZLAFF, 1967
THE SPORTING NEWS

"YOU LOOK AT THE BEST
TEAMS IN THE LEAGUE
AND THEY ALL HAVE
RECEIVERS LIKE ART. HE
IS SO DANGEROUS AT ALL
TIMES. HE BREAKS INTO
THE SEAM, GETS ONE
STEP ON HIS MAN AND
WATCH OUT."

FORMER REDSKINS COACH
JACK PARDEE, 1980

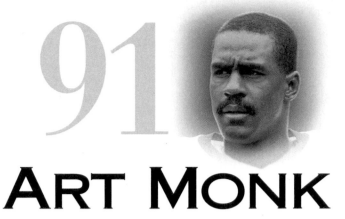

91
ART MONK

His name rolls off the tongue softly, quietly, befitting the man it identifies. Art Monk is almost as proud of his relative anonymity as he is the record-setting numbers he compiled over a 16-year NFL career. He was Washington's Quiet Man, the go-to wide receiver for four Super Bowl teams. When Monk spoke, it was usually with tough catches in the clutch moments of big games.

Big (6-3, 210) and physical, Monk was a wide receiver in a tight end's body. Unable to dazzle anybody with his speed, he became a route-running technician who would go outside or inside with fearless defiance. Nobody was more consistent on medium routes over the middle, football's no-man's land of broken ribs and shattered careers. Third down and other key situations belonged to Monk, who turned cornerbacks around with his quick moves and long, graceful stride. He also was adept at positioning his large body to seal off smaller defensive backs before gathering the ball.

Nothing came naturally for Monk, who spent countless hours on the practice field and many more behind the projector. The workmanlike dedication paid off in consistency and earned the appreciation of understanding Redskins fans. Monk, who spent most of his career trying to avoid the spotlight, gained reluctant acclaim in 1984 when he caught 106 passes, a season record that stood for eight years, and in 1992 when he passed Steve Largent and temporarily became the all-time receptions leader.

Throughout a career that ended in Philadelphia in 1995 and produced 940 catches for 12,721 yards and 68 touchdowns, Monk was seldom mentioned among superstar receivers. Despite five 1,000-yard seasons and a then-record 183 straight games with at least one catch, he was named to only three Pro Bowl teams. But those who worked with Monk appreciated his value. "Quiet about his work, very loud with his results," former Redskins quarterback Mark Rypien said.

TOUGHEST RECEIVERS TO COVER
SELECTED BY RONNIE LOTT

1. Jerry Rice	6. Steve Largent
2. John Jefferson	7. Mark Clayton
3. Art Monk	8. Charlie Joiner
4. James Lofton	9. Wes Chandler
5. Andre Reed	10. Kellen Winslow

"FOUTS IS SO TOUGH, SO VERY TOUGH.
AND I THINK HE IMPARTS THAT TOUGHNESS
TO THE REST OF THE TEAM. THEY SEE
HE'LL DO ANYTHING TO WIN AND THEY
GO OUT THERE AND PLAY THE SAME WAY."

FORMER CHARGERS
OFFENSIVE COORDINATOR
JOE GIBBS, 1980
THE SPORTING NEWS

92

DAN FOUTS

H e was ringmaster of the aerial circus known as "Air Coryell," the passing fancy in a prolific offense that threw the ball first and asked questions later. Defenses braced for the inevitable onslaught

and fans gasped in anticipation when Dan Fouts took the field. He might not have fit the classic quarterback mold, but there's no denying the 43,040 yards and 254 touchdown passes he delivered over a 15-year career with the San Diego Chargers.

At first glance, Fouts fell short of the job description. His 6-3, 204-pound body did not look athletic, his arm was ordinary and he was painfully slow. But closer inspection revealed a super-quick release and a feathery touch that dropped passes between the seams in zones. Fouts was a master at the quick-hitting pattern, but he also had extraordinary peripheral vision and stood fearlessly in the pocket, waiting for someone to get open as the world collapsed around him.

Teammates marveled at the presence Fouts brought to the huddle. All was quiet

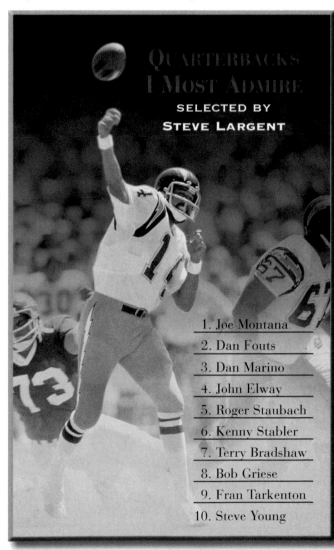

QUARTERBACKS
I MOST ADMIRE

SELECTED BY
STEVE LARGENT

1. Joe Montana
2. Dan Fouts
3. Dan Marino
4. John Elway
5. Roger Staubach
6. Kenny Stabler
7. Terry Bradshaw
8. Bob Griese
9. Fran Tarkenton
10. Steve Young

when he barked orders in an I'm-in-charge tone that commanded respect. His intense personality sometimes grated on teammates, but nobody doubted his competitive fire and desire to succeed—a desire that would not be fulfilled until Don Coryell brought his wide-open offense to San Diego in 1978.

That's when Fouts began piling up yards— and points—in bunches. Throwing to Charlic Joiner, John Jefferson and Kellen Winslow in 1979, Fouts passed for a season-record 4,082 yards. He followed that with seasons of 4,715 and 4,802 yards and never fell below the 2,500-yard level over the rest of a career that ended in 1987. Fouts, a six-time Pro Bowl selection, never led his team to the championship he craved, but he did get the Chargers to the AFC title game after the 1980 and '81 seasons.

"MIKE HAYNES IS A SPECIAL PLAYER.
HE JUST HAS ABILITY OTHER PLAYERS
DON'T HAVE."

FORMER PATRIOTS COACH
CHUCK FAIRBANKS, 1977
THE SPORTING NEWS

93

MIKE HAYNES

A Sunday afternoon with Mike Haynes was a bonding experience. He didn't limit his introductions to a few well-timed hits or an occasional takedown. When NFL wide receivers got together with the friendliest cornerback in the game, they usually shared a single jersey for 60 excruciating minutes. Haynes was a smothering presence, the shadow that wouldn't go away.

Few corners in football history played tighter than Haynes, who was an impressive package of speed, quickness and size. The 6-2, 192-pound Haynes was a man-to-man demon who frustrated receivers from his 1976 debut with the New England Patriots to his 1989 final season with the Los Angeles Raiders. His coverage skills were so intimidating to offenses that Patriots coach Chuck Fairbanks once remarked, "Mike hasn't seen a ball come his way in over three weeks."

It wasn't that way when Haynes picked off eight passes in a big rookie season that also included two punt returns for touchdowns. It didn't take long for

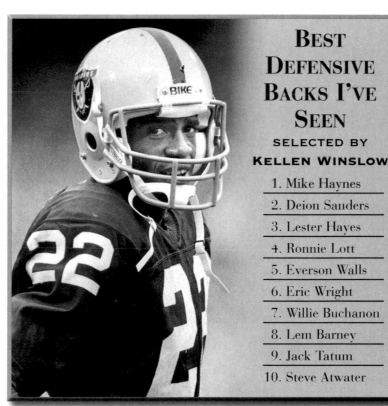

BEST DEFENSIVE BACKS I'VE SEEN

SELECTED BY KELLEN WINSLOW

1. Mike Haynes
2. Deion Sanders
3. Lester Hayes
4. Ronnie Lott
5. Everson Walls
6. Eric Wright
7. Willie Buchanon
8. Lem Barney
9. Jack Tatum
10. Steve Atwater

Haynes to become known as a thinking man's defensive back, a worker who relentlessly studied film and rehearsed his moves based on opponents' tendencies. Totally prepared for what he might see on Sunday afternoons, he seldom fell for fakes or moves that normally would separate the good receiver from his shadow.

The reputation grew in New England, but a 1983 move to Los Angeles really vaulted Haynes into a national spotlight. He teamed with the more-physical Lester Hayes from 1983 to '86 as one of the best cornerback tandems in pro football history and he played a big part in the Raiders' Super Bowl XVIII pounding of the Washington Redskins. The nine-time Pro Bowl selection, also known as an electrifying runner after picking off passes, finished his 14-year career with 46 interceptions.

94

FRED BILETNIKOFF

Discussions about Fred Biletnikoff inevitably start with the hands—big, soft, supple and covered with the gooey substance he called "stickum." They were amazing hands, ball-attracting magnets that pulled in any pass within the time zone of his pattern. If Biletnikoff could touch a ball, he could catch it—a fact he proved over and over during a 14-year AFL/NFL journey that started in Oakland and ended in the Hall of Fame.

Biletnikoff wasn't fast and his narrow-shouldered, 190-pound frame should by all rights have disintegrated with the heavy pounding it absorbed from 1965 to '78, when Biletnikoff turned sideline and over-the-middle pass catching into an art form. He couldn't beat the faster defensive backs physically, but he could outwork and outthink them. Biletnikoff's precise, perfectly timed, sleight-of-foot patterns became legendary, as did his ability to make the difficult catch at the crucial point of a game.

Nothing came easy for Biletnikoff, who studied reels of film before every game and spent hours catching practice passes. The work habits were born from chronic worry, which was responsible for the ulcer he developed during his college days at Florida State. He agonized, paced and threw up before every game, and it took hours for him to calm down afterward. He was enraged, absolutely mortified, by every dropped pass.

With quarterbacks Daryle Lamonica and Ken Stabler throwing to him, Biletnikoff thrived as the clutch, big-game possession receiver. The Raiders never had a losing season during his career and he played in three AFL championship games, six AFC title games and two Super Bowls, including a Super Bowl XI victory over Minnesota in which he earned MVP honors. A six-time Pro Bowl choice, he topped 40 catches for 10 straight seasons and 100 yards in a game 21 times.

TOUGHEST RECEIVERS TO COVER

SELECTED BY **LEM BARNEY**

1. Paul Warfield
2. Fred Biletnikoff
3. Charlie Joiner
4. Art Monk
5. Tim Brown
6. Bobby Mitchell
7. Charley Taylor
8. Jerry Rice
9. Cris Carter
10. Steve Largent

"HE WAS A DECEPTIVE RECEIVER. EVERYBODY SAID HE WAS SLOW, BUT HE ALWAYS SEEMED TO GET BEHIND PEOPLE. HE WAS VERY FLUID. HE USED THAT STICKUM ON HIS HANDS AND STUCK HIS WAY INTO THE HALL OF FAME."

LEM BARNEY, 1999

95

TROY AIKMAN

The last place you'll find Troy Aikman is at the top of the career passing yards chart. And don't look for him among the most prolific touchdown throwers, scramblers or comeback quarterbacks. But if

you want to talk Super Bowl championships or completion percentage or leadership qualities, then book a flight for Dallas and an interview with America's Quarterback.

With Aikman, it's all about efficiency and winning. He's the prototypical quarterback with size (6-4, 219 pounds), a great arm and incredible accuracy, so good that scouts marvel at the precision and consistency with which he delivers passes to appreciative receivers. But because of a balanced Cowboys offense that relies heavily on Emmitt Smith and a controlled, structured passing scheme, he has been forced into a system-dictated field-general role, reliant on his impressive skills as decision-maker and strategist.

That's all right with the soft-spoken Aikman, who has pulled the strings for six NFC East titles and three Super Bowl

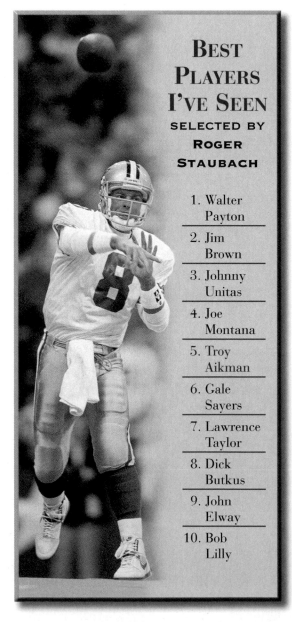

BEST PLAYERS I'VE SEEN

SELECTED BY
ROGER STAUBACH

1. Walter Payton
2. Jim Brown
3. Johnny Unitas
4. Joe Montana
5. Troy Aikman
6. Gale Sayers
7. Lawrence Taylor
8. Dick Butkus
9. John Elway
10. Bob Lilly

winners since his NFL arrival in 1989. He's tough, competitive and capable of posting big numbers in a high-powered passing attack but has settled for winning while sharing the spotlight with superstar teammates Smith, Michael Irvin, Larry Allen and Deion Sanders.

Aikman, whose steely blue eyes and stoic facade belie his fiery on-field demeanor, is a straight dropback passer whose field savvy elevates the players around him. An Aikman-led offense is like a clock that is always on time, ready to strike on cue and never out of sync despite mayhem all around. The six-time Pro Bowl selection enters the 1999 season with a career .618 completion percentage, one of the top figures in football history. His 82.8 passer rating is ninth all-time, just behind former Cowboy Roger Staubach's 83.4.

"YOU CAN FIND FAULTS IN
OTHER PEOPLE, BUT WHEN YOU
LOOK AT TROY, HE HAS NONE.
YOU SEE HOW A QUARTERBACK
IS SUPPOSED TO PLAY. HE IS
QUICK WITH HIS STEP, HE
THROWS WITH PERFECT FORM,
HE MAKES THE DIFFICULT
PASSES LOOK EASY, HE MAKES
GREAT DECISIONS."

SONNY JURGENSEN, 1996
THE SPORTING NEWS

96

JOE NAMATH

There were imperfections: a stoop-shouldered slouch, spindly legs and knees held together by rubber bands. But the rest of Joe Willie Namath was a masterpiece, from his long black hair, million-dollar

smile and white shoes to the roguish charm he dispensed in large doses. And there was that arm, the weapon he used to dazzle fans and destroy secondaries for 13 pro seasons, all but one at center stage with the New York Jets.

Brash, bold, cocky, flamboyant, stylish—all the adjectives applied to Broadway Joe, who never met a party he didn't like or a defensive back he couldn't beat. He began his love affair with New York when he rejected NFL overtures in 1965 and signed a stunning contract with the AFL's Jets. And he shocked the football world four years later when he took the Jets to Super Bowl III, brashly predicted a victory over heavily favored Baltimore—and delivered.

That victory captured the essence of Namath, the fun-loving playboy who brought instant respect to the AFL and credibility to the still-young Super Bowl series. He was one of those rare athletes who affected the game in ways that far exceeded his accomplishments. Everyone remembers the leadership, clever play-calling and excitement he brought to every game, but it was the superstar aura, the near-perfect passing form, the needle-threading throws and

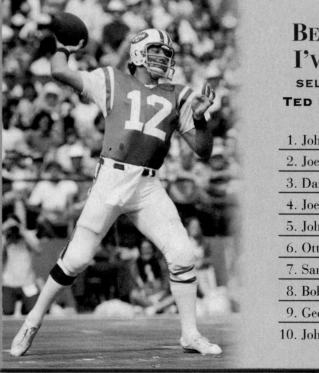

BEST QBS I'VE SEEN
SELECTED BY TED HENDRICKS

| 1. Johnny Unitas |
| 2. Joe Namath |
| 3. Dan Marino |
| 4. Joe Montana |
| 5. John Elway |
| 6. Otto Graham |
| 7. Sammy Baugh |
| 8. Bobby Layne |
| 9. George Blanda |
| 10. John Brodie |

the I-can-do-anything swagger that set him apart.

Namath's Super Bowl moment was complemented by a steady stream of 300- and 400-yard passing games and the first 4,000-yard season (1967) in history. But the bad knees and other injuries took a toll, as did weak Jets teams that failed to post a winning record after 1969 during the Namath era. The five-time Pro Bowl selection retired after one injury-plagued season (1977) with the Los Angeles Rams.

"HE CAN REALLY WING THAT BALL IN THERE. HE HAS STRENGTH AND ACCURACY AND YOU'D BETTER GET TO HIM OR HE WILL RUN YOU OUT OF THE PARK. HE ALREADY IS IN A CLASS BY HIMSELF."

FORMER BENGALS COACH PAUL BROWN

97

LEM BARNEY

The legs churned furiously, transporting a twisting, squirming body in its mad search for daylight. Watching a dazzling Lem Barney runback was worth the price of admission. Then, when his sprinter's speed had separated him from the pack, he would slow down to cruise control, look back and wave to his pursuers, a theatrical maneuver that delighted Detroit fans and infuriated frustrated opponents.

It was clear from his first play in 1967 that Barney was something special, a worthy successor at left cornerback to the just-retired Dick "Night Train" Lane. Barney picked off a pass from Green Bay's Bart Starr with a diving somersault, jumped to his feet and sprinted 24 yards for a touchdown. It was the first of 10 rookie interceptions and an auspicious beginning to an 11-year career that would net 56 pickoffs, seven for TDs.

Packers wide receiver Carroll Dale once said, "The only way to beat him is to be perfect," and sometimes that wasn't even enough. Barney (6-0, 188) was a physical, bump-and-run ballhawk who would lay back and then use superior quickness to jump into the play. Like Lane, he was a confident gambler and big-play artist who also attacked the run with furious anticipation. Barney was so proficient at one-on-one

ALL-TIME INTERCEPTION AVERAGE
(BASED ON 50 OR MORE INTERCEPTIONS)

Rk. Name	No.	Avg.
1. Lem Barney	56	19.2
2. Bobby Dillon	52	18.8
3. Night Train Lane	68	17.8
4. Bobby Boyd	57	17.4
5. Pat Fischer	56	16.8
6. Emlen Tunnell	79	16.2
7. Emmitt Thomas	58	16.2
8. Jack Butler	52	15.9
9. Larry Wilson	52	15.4
10. Paul Krause	81	14.6

coverage that the Lions were able to blitz a lot.

Barney seemed to be happiest when displaying his "sneaky and snaky" moves on runbacks of punts and interceptions. It was like trying to catch a lightning bug as he darted in and out of traffic—a style that produced four career runbacks of 70 or more yards. Understandably, he became a fan favorite for weak Detroit teams that made one brief playoff appearance before he retired in 1977 after seven Pro Bowl selections.

98

GEORGE BLANDA

"BLANDA HAD A GOD-GIVEN KILLER INSTINCT TO MAKE IT HAPPEN WHEN EVERYTHING WAS ON THE LINE. I REALLY BELIEVE THAT GEORGE BLANDA IS THE GREATEST CLUTCH PLAYER I HAVE EVER SEEN IN THE HISTORY OF PRO FOOTBALL."

AL DAVIS, 1987
THE SPORTING NEWS

We always will remember the long, gray hair and the well-lined face. George Blanda never got old, he just got better. Over 26 incredible pro seasons, he posted a record 2,002 points and an impressive 236 touchdown passes as a kicker and quarterback. But the real legacy of George Blanda is the magic he created as an American folk hero who continued to deliver clutch performances in his fourth football decade, until the age of 48.

Through much of his career, Blanda was a backup quarterback and full-time kicker with a straight-on, confident and accurate stroke. That confidence carried over to his quarterback duties, which he executed with a veteran savvy that overcame limited arm strength and lack of speed. Blanda was a scoring machine for 10 years as a Chicago Bears kicker, an icy competitor when he finally got his first call as a long-term starting quarterback and led Houston to championships in the AFL's first two seasons. Blanda fired 36 touchdown passes in 1961, seven in one game.

But nothing could match the dramatic impact Blanda brought to the Oakland Raiders from 1967 until his 1975 retirement as the oldest player in football history. In a magic 1970 season, at age 43, the Old Man came off the bench in five straight games to deliver a dramatic kick or touchdown pass that produced a win or tie. The heroics continued in subsequent seasons as the blazing blue eyes, protruding jaw and craggy face of No. 16 became a highlight-film regular.

Blanda was a popular, sometimes-testy leader who played in a record 340 games. He was the epitome of the grizzled veteran, the symbol of everlasting youth. It's no coincidence that the determined, unflappable Blanda played in one Super Bowl and 11 AFL/NFL championship games in a career that produced 335 field goals, 943 extra points and 26,920 passing yards.

BEST PLAYERS I'VE SEEN
SELECTED BY LEM BARNEY

1. Deacon Jones
2. Jim Brown
3. Barry Sanders
4. Walter Payton
5. George Blanda
6. Dick Butkus
7. John Mackey
8. Gale Sayers
9. Roger Staubach
10. Joe Namath

99
LOU GROZA

"ANYWHERE FROM 40 OR 50 YARDS, HE WAS A WEAPON. FOR A STRAIGHT-ON KICKER, HE WAS VERY ACCURATE. HE HAD A STRONG LEG."

LONGTIME GROZA HOLDER TOMMY JAMES, 1999

He was known as The Toe, a nickname he lived up to every day for 21 professional seasons. Lou Groza was a place-kicking pioneer who just happened to double as an All-Pro-caliber offensive tackle.

He could open up holes for the Cleveland Browns' machine-like offense and then cap a drive with a 40-yard field goal. He represented a distinct point-producing advantage for the Browns in the era of 33-man rosters.

Groza was pro football's first great kicker, and his strong right leg and trademark black high-tops left a long-term imprint on the game. He was automatic on extra points and everyone marveled at his accuracy from as far away as midfield. He approached his craft scientifically, working constantly on technique while measuring off precise steps and distances. He became so proficient that Cleveland coach Paul Brown began using him as a fourth-down field-goal option, a huge plus in an era where field goals were not frequently attempted.

Groza, who spent his college years fighting in World War II, was part of Brown's master plan when he constructed the Cleveland franchise that would dominate the new All-America Football Conference from 1946-49 and the NFL through much of the 1950s. Not only did the 6-3, 240-pounder give the Browns a kicking-game edge, he contributed as a solid run-blocking tackle for 14 seasons before concentrating strictly on placements. By the time he retired after the 1967 season, Groza held virtually every NFL kicking record and had totaled 1,608 professional points.

The personable, always-popular Groza succeeded in the trenches without the warrior mentality of the normal lineman. His secret was technique and coolness under pressure, which was front and center in 1950 when he kicked a 16-yard field goal with 28 seconds remaining to give the Browns a 30-28 victory over the Los Angeles Rams and their first NFL championship.

TOP 10 ALL-TIME SCORERS

(COMBINED AFL, AAFC AND NFL TOTALS)

Rk. Name	Pts.
1. George Blanda	2,002
2. Gary Anderson	1,845
3. Morten Andersen	1,761
4. Nick Lowery	1,711
5. Jan Stenerud	1,699
6. Norm Johnson	1,657
7. Lou Groza	1,608
8. Eddie Murray	1,532
9. Pat Leahy	1,470
10. Jim Turner	1,439

100

CHARLIE JOINER

He was a football scientist, a technician with a plan. When Charlie Joiner stepped on the field, he wanted everything precise and exact. That's the way he ran his pass patterns for 18 NFL seasons and that's the way he dissected defenses as one of the premier possession receivers in league history.

Bill Walsh, who coached Joiner at Cincinnati and San Diego, called him "the most intelligent and perceptive receiver the game has ever seen." And that sentiment was shared by numerous defensive backs, who watched the former Grambling star slip into the seams of zones and catch pass after pass. Nobody was better at reading defenses, a skill he tried to pass on to younger teammates, and few have found those seams with more consistency. He was simply a model of reliability, a fact much appreciated by his quarterbacks, particularly Dan Fouts.

At first glance, Joiner appeared to be too small (5-11, 188) and too docile to make an impact in the NFL. But the calm, thoughtful, private demeanor players saw in the locker room turned into fiery, hustling competitiveness that complemented the intelligence he used to break down defenders. The always well-conditioned Joiner had quick feet, great body control and the ability to break into the open at a precisely planned moment.

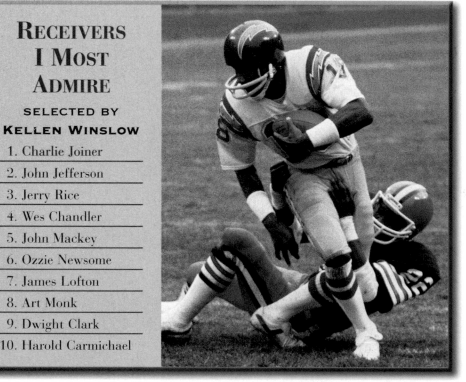

RECEIVERS I MOST ADMIRE

SELECTED BY KELLEN WINSLOW

1. Charlie Joiner
2. John Jefferson
3. Jerry Rice
4. Wes Chandler
5. John Mackey
6. Ozzie Newsome
7. James Lofton
8. Art Monk
9. Dwight Clark
10. Harold Carmichael

Joiner's career really blossomed in 1976, when he was traded to San Diego after seven years with run-oriented Houston and Cincinnati teams. But the Chargers' Air Coryell attack, featuring Fouts throwing to such receivers as Joiner, John Jefferson, Wes Chandler and Kellen Winslow, was a perfect fit and Joiner caught 586 passes for 9,203 yards and 47 touchdowns over his final 11 seasons. When the three-time Pro Bowl choice retired in 1986, he was the most prolific receiver of all time (750 career catches), a record that was broken by Steve Largent a year later.

"I KNOW WHERE HE WILL BE.
I KNOW WHAT HE WILL DO.
I KNOW IF I GET THE BALL
TO HIM, HE WILL CATCH IT.
WHAT MORE CAN YOU SAY?"

DAN FOUTS, 1983
THE SPORTING NEWS

BY POSITION

The following list shows the position breakdowns for the Top 100 players. Seven players are listed at two positions and two more, Sammy Baugh and Sid Luckman, at three. Other members of the list were two-way players for only brief periods. Bronko Nagurski played several offensive positions but is known primarily as a fullback.

Quarterbacks (18): Troy Aikman, Sammy Baugh*, George Blanda*, Terry Bradshaw, John Elway, Brett Favre, Dan Fouts, Otto Graham, Bobby Layne, Sid Luckman*, Dan Marino, Joe Montana, Joe Namath, Bart Starr, Roger Staubach, Fran Tarkenton, Johnny Unitas, Steve Young.

Running backs (17): Marcus Allen, Jim Brown, Earl Campbell, Eric Dickerson, Tony Dorsett, Red Grange*, Franco Harris, Lenny Moore, Marion Motley, Bronko Nagurski*, Walter Payton, Barry Sanders, Gale Sayers, O.J. Simpson, Emmitt Smith, Jim Thorpe, Steve Van Buren.

Wide receivers (11): Lance Alworth, Raymond Berry, Fred Biletnikoff, Don Hutson*, Elroy Hirsch, Charlie Joiner, Steve Largent, Art Monk, Jerry Rice, Charley Taylor, Paul Warfield.

Tight ends (3): Mike Ditka, John Mackey, Kellen Winslow.

Offensive linemen (14): Chuck Bednarik*, Roosevelt Brown, Forrest Gregg, Lou Groza*, John Hannah, Mel Hein*, Larry Little, Anthony Munoz, Jim Otto, Jim Parker, Art Shell, Dwight Stephenson, Gene Upshaw, Mike Webster.

Defensive linemen (11): Buck Buchanan, Willie Davis, Joe Greene, Deacon Jones, Bob Lilly, Gino Marchetti, Merlin Olsen, Alan Page, Bruce Smith, Randy White, Reggie White.

Linebackers (15): Chuck Bednarik*, Bobby Bell, Dick Butkus, Bill George, Jack Ham, Mel Hein*, Ted Hendricks, Sam Huff, Jack Lambert, Willie Lanier, Bronko Nagurski*, Ray Nitschke, Joe Schmidt, Mike Singletary, Lawrence Taylor.

Defensive backs (18): Herb Adderley, Lem Barney, Sammy Baugh*, Mel Blount, Willie Brown, Jack Christiansen, Red Grange*, Darrell Green, Mike Haynes, Ken Houston, Don Hutson*, Night Train Lane, Ronnie Lott, Sid Luckman*, Deion Sanders, Emlen Tunnell, Larry Wilson, Rod Woodson.

Punters (2): Sammy Baugh*, Sid Luckman*.

Kickers (2): George Blanda*, Lou Groza*.

*Listed at more than one position.

Barry Sanders

BY COLLEGE

The following list breaks down the colleges of the Top 100 players.

Alabama (5): John Hannah, Don Hutson, Joe Namath, Bart Starr, Dwight Stephenson.

Arizona State (2): Mike Haynes, Charley Taylor.

Arkansas (1): Lance Alworth.

Baylor (1): Mike Singletary.

Bethune-Cookman (1): Larry Little.

Brigham Young (1): Steve Young.

Carlisle (1): Jim Thorpe.

Colorado A&M (1): Jack Christiansen.

Columbia (1): Sid Luckman.

Florida (1): Emmitt Smith.

Florida State (2): Fred Biletnikoff, Deion Sanders.

Georgia (1): Fran Tarkenton.

Grambling State (4): Willie Brown, Buck Buchanan, Willie Davis, Charlie Joiner.

Illinois (3): Dick Butkus, Red Grange, Ray Nitschke.

Iowa (1): Emlen Tunnell.

Jackson State (2): Lem Barney, Walter Payton.

Kansas (1): Gale Sayers.

Kent State (1): Jack Lambert.

Kentucky (1): George Blanda.

Louisiana State (1): Steve Van Buren.

Louisiana Tech (1): Terry Bradshaw.

Louisville (1): Johnny Unitas.

Maryland (1): Randy White.

Maryland-Eastern Shore (1): Art Shell.

Miami (Fla.) (2): Ted Hendricks, Jim Otto.

Michigan State (1): Herb Adderley.

Minnesota (2): Bobby Bell, Bronko Nagurski.

Missouri (1): Kellen Winslow.

Mississippi Valley State (1): Jerry Rice.

Morgan State (2): Roosevelt Brown, Willie Lanier.

Navy (1): Roger Staubach.

Nevada (1): Marion Motley.

North Carolina (1): Lawrence Taylor.

North Texas State (1): Joe Greene.

Northwestern (1): Otto Graham.

BREAKDOWNS

BY PRIMARY TEAMS

The following list breaks down the primary teams of the Top 100 players, with game totals in parentheses next to the player names. Players need 48 or more games to qualify for a team's roster. The list does not include Jim Thorpe, who played for six different teams in his eight-year career and did not qualify for a roster.

Atlanta Falcons (1): Deion Sanders* (70).

Baltimore/Indianapolis Colts (8): Raymond Berry (154); Eric Dickerson* (61); Ted Hendricks* (70); John Mackey (126); Gino Marchetti (149); Lenny Moore (143); Jim Parker (135); Johnny Unitas (206).

Buffalo Bills (2): O.J. Simpson (112); Bruce Smith (201).

Chicago Bears (12): George Blanda* (115); Dick Butkus (119); Mike Ditka* (84); Bill George (159); Red Grange (83); Night Train Lane* (68); Sid Luckman (128); Bronko Nagurski (97); Alan Page* (58); Walter Payton (190); Gale Sayers (68); Mike Singletary (179).

Cincinnati Bengals (1): Anthony Munoz (185).

Cleveland Browns (5): Jim Brown (118); Otto Graham (126); Lou Groza (268); Marion Motley (99); Paul Warfield* (97).

Dallas Cowboys (8): Troy Aikman (140); Mike Ditka* (54); Tony Dorsett (156); Bob Lilly (196); Deion Sanders* (49); Emmitt Smith (140); Roger Staubach (131); Randy White (209).

Denver Broncos (2): Willie Brown* (50); John Elway (234).

Detroit Lions (6): Lem Barney (140); Jack Christiansen (89); Night Train Lane* (66); Bobby Layne* (97); Barry Sanders (153); Joe Schmidt (155).

Green Bay Packers (8): Herb Adderley (125); Willie Davis (138); Brett Favre (111); Forrest Gregg (187); Don Hutson (116); Ray Nitschke (190); Bart Starr (196); Reggie White* (95).

Houston/Tennessee Oilers (3): George Blanda* (98); Earl Campbell (91); Ken Houston* (84).

Kansas City Chiefs (4): Marcus Allen* (77); Bobby Bell (168); Buck Buchanan (182); Willie Lanier (149).

Cleveland/Los Angeles/St. Louis Rams (4): Eric Dickerson* (65); Elroy Hirsch (103); Deacon Jones (151); Merlin Olsen (208).

Miami Dolphins (4): Larry Little (159); Dan Marino (231); Dwight Stephenson (114); Paul Warfield* (60).

Minnesota Vikings (2): Alan Page* (160); Fran Tarkenton* (177).

New England Patriots (2): John Hannah (183); Mike Haynes* (90).

New York Giants (6): Roosevelt Brown (163); Mel Hein (170); Sam Huff* (102); Fran Tarkenton* (69); Lawrence Taylor (184); Emlen Tunnell (130).

New York Jets (1): Joe Namath (136).

Oakland/Los Angeles Raiders (9): Marcus Allen* (144); Fred Biletnikoff (190); George Blanda* (126); Willie Brown* (154); Mike Haynes* (87); Ted Hendricks* (131); Jim Otto (210); Art Shell (207); Gene Upshaw (217).

Philadelphia Eagles (3): Chuck Bednarik (169); Steve Van Buren (83); Reggie White* (121).

Pittsburgh Steelers (9): Mel Blount (200); Terry Bradshaw (168); Joe Greene (181); Jack Ham (162); Franco Harris (165); Jack Lambert (146); Bobby Layne* (55); Mike Webster (220); Rod Woodson (134).

Chicago/St. Louis/Arizona Cardinals (1): Larry Wilson (169).

San Diego Chargers (4): Lance Alworth (110); Dan Fouts (181); Charlie Joiner (164); Kellen Winslow (109).

San Francisco 49ers (4): Ronnie Lott (129); Joe Montana (167); Jerry Rice (206); Steve Young (147).

Seattle Seahawks (1): Steve Largent (200).

Washington Redskins (6): Sammy Baugh (165); Darrell Green (234); Ken Houston* (112); Sam Huff* (66); Art Monk (205); Charley Taylor (165).

*Listed with more than one team.

Troy Aikman

Notre Dame (2): Joe Montana, Alan Page.
Ohio State (3): Lou Groza, Jim Parker, Paul Warfield.
Oklahoma State (1): Barry Sanders.
Oregon (1): Dan Fouts.
Pennsylvania (1): Chuck Bednarik.
Penn State (3): Jack Ham, Franco Harris, Lenny Moore.
Pittsburgh (4): Mike Ditka, Tony Dorsett, Dan Marino, Joe Schmidt.
Prairie View A&M (1): Ken Houston.
Purdue (1): Rod Woodson.
San Francisco (1): Gino Marchetti.
Scottsbluff JC (1): Night Train Lane.
Southern (La.) (1): Mel Blount.
SMU (3): Raymond Berry, Eric Dickerson, Forrest Gregg.
South Carolina State (1): Deacon Jones.
USC (4): Marcus Allen, Ronnie Lott, Anthony Munoz, O.J. Simpson.
Southern Mississippi (1): Brett Favre.
Stanford (1): John Elway.
Syracuse (3): Jim Brown, John Mackey, Art Monk.
Tennessee (1): Reggie White.
Texas (2): Earl Campbell, Bobby Layne.
Texas A&I (2): Darrell Green, Gene Upshaw.
Texas Christian (2): Sammy Baugh, Bob Lilly.
Tulsa (1): Steve Largent.
UCLA (1): Troy Aikman.
Utah (1): Larry Wilson.
Utah State (1): Merlin Olsen.
Virginia Tech (1): Bruce Smith.
Wake Forest (1): Bill George.
Washington State (1): Mel Hein.
West Virginia (1): Sam Huff.
Wisconsin (2): Elroy Hirsch, Mike Webster.

By Birthdates

JANUARY
2—Gino Marchetti (1927)
5—Jim Otto (1938)
9—Bart Starr (1934)
15—Randy White (1953)
18—Joe Schmidt (1932)
25—Lou Groza (1924)
31—Don Hutson (1913)

FEBRUARY
3—Fran Tarkenton (1940)
4—Lawrence Taylor (1959)
5—Roger Staubach (1942)
15—Darrell Green (1960)
17—Jim Brown (1936)
23—Fred Biletnikoff (1943)
27—Raymond Berry (1933)

MARCH
7—Franco Harris (1950)
10—Rod Woodson (1965)
17—Sammy Baugh (1914)
18—Mike Webster (1952)
24—Larry Wilson (1938)
26—Marcus Allen (1960)
29—Emlen Tunnell (1922);
Earl Campbell (1955)

APRIL
3—Jim Parker (1934)
4—John Hannah (1951)
7—Tony Dorsett (1954)
10—Mel Blount (1948)
16—Night Train Lane (1928)

MAY
1—Chuck Bednarik (1925)
7—Johnny Unitas (1933)
8—Ronnie Lott (1959)
15—Emmitt Smith (1969)
28—Jim Thorpe (1887)
30—Gale Sayers (1943)
31—Joe Namath (1943)

JUNE
5—Marion Motley (1920)
8—Herb Adderley (1939)
10—Dan Fouts (1951)
11—Joe Montana (1956)
13—Red Grange (1903)
17—Elroy Hirsch (1923);
Bobby Bell (1940)
18—Bruce Smith (1963)
28—John Elway (1960)

JULY
1—Mike Haynes (1953)
8—Jack Lambert (1952)
9—O.J. Simpson (1947)
16—Barry Sanders (1968)
24—Willie Davis (1934)
25—Walter Payton (1954)
26—Bob Lilly (1939)

AUGUST
3—Lance Alworth (1940)
7—Alan Page (1945)
9—Deion Sanders (1967)
15—Gene Upshaw (1945)
19—Anthony Munoz (1958)
21—Willie Lanier (1945)
22—Mel Hein (1909)

SEPTEMBER
2—Terry Bradshaw (1948);
Eric Dickerson (1960)
8—Lem Barney (1945)
10—Buck Buchanan (1940)
15—Merlin Olsen (1940);
Dan Marino (1961)
17—George Blanda (1927)
24—John Mackey (1941);
Joe Greene (1946)
28—Charley Taylor (1941);
Steve Largent (1954)

OCTOBER
4—Sam Huff (1934)
9—Mike Singletary (1958)
10—Brett Favre (1969)
11—Steve Young (1961)
13—Jerry Rice (1962)
14—Charlie Joiner (1947)
18—Forrest Gregg (1933);
Mike Ditka (1939)
20—Roosevelt Brown (1932)
27—Bill George (1929)

NOVEMBER
1—Ted Hendricks (1947)
2—Larry Little (1945)
3—Bronko Nagurski (1908)
5—Kellen Winslow (1957)
12—Ken Houston (1944)
20—Dwight Stephenson (1957)
21—Sid Luckman (1916);
Troy Aikman (1966)
25—Lenny Moore (1933)
26—Art Shell (1946)
28—Paul Warfield (1942)

DECEMBER
2—Willie Brown (1940)
5—Art Monk (1957)
6—Otto Graham (1921)
9—Deacon Jones (1938);
Dick Butkus (1942)
19—Bobby Layne (1926);
Reggie White (1961)
20—Jack Christiansen (1928)
23—Jack Ham (1948)
28—Steve Van Buren (1920)
29—Ray Nitschke (1936)

By Birthplaces

The following list breaks down the states and cities in which the Top 100 players were born.

ALABAMA (2): Buck Buchanan (Gainesville); Bart Starr (Montgomery).

ARKANSAS (1): Don Hutson (Pine Bluff).

CALIFORNIA (6): Troy Aikman (West Covina); Marcus Allen (San Diego); Dan Fouts (San Francisco); Mel Hein (Redding); Anthony Munoz (Ontario); O.J. Simpson (San Francisco).

DELAWARE: (1) Randy White (Wilmington).

FLORIDA (3): Deacon Jones (Eatonville); Deion Sanders (Fort Myers); Emmitt Smith (Pensacola).

GEORGIA (6): Mel Blount (Vidalia); Jim Brown (St. Simons Island); John Hannah (Canton); Larry Little (Groveland); Marion Motley (Leesburg); Jim Parker (Macon).

IDAHO (1): Larry Wilson (Rigby).

ILLINOIS (3): Dick Butkus (Chicago); Otto Graham (Waukegan); Ray Nitschke (Elmwood Park).

INDIANA (1): Rod Woodson (Fort Wayne).

KANSAS (3): Jack Christiansen (Sublette); Barry Sanders (Wichita); Gale Sayers (Wichita).

LOUISIANA (3): Terry Bradshaw (Shreveport); Willie Davis (Lisbon); Charlie Joiner (Many).

TOP 100

By Seasons/Games Played

The following list breaks down the Top 100 players by seasons played with total games in parentheses. Note: The totals for Otto Graham, Elroy Hirsch, Marion Motley and Lou Groza combine AAFC and NFL service. All other totals reflect only AFL/NFL numbers. Totals are through the 1998 season.

26—George Blanda (340).

21—Lou Groza (268).

18—Charlie Joiner (239); Fran Tarkenton (246); Johnny Unitas (211).

17—Mike Webster (245).

16—Marcus Allen (221); Sammy Baugh (165); Willie Brown (204); John Elway (234); Darrell Green (234); Dan Marino (231); Art Monk (224); Bart Starr (196).

15—Dan Fouts (181); Bill George (173); Forrest Gregg (193); Mel Hein (170); Ted Hendricks (215); Bobby Layne (175); Joe Montana (192); Ray Nitschke (190); Merlin Olsen (208); Jim Otto (210); Alan Page (218); Art Shell (207); Gene Upshaw (217).

14—Chuck Bednarik (169); Fred Biletnikoff (190); Mel Blount (200); Terry Bradshaw (168); Mike Haynes

MISSISSIPPI (5): Lem Barney (Gulfport); Willie Brown (Yazoo City); Brett Favre (Pass Christian); Walter Payton (Columbia); Jerry Rice (Starkville).

MISSOURI (1): Kellen Winslow (St. Louis).

NEW JERSEY (1): Franco Harris (Mount Holly).

NEW MEXICO (1): Ronnie Lott (Albuquerque).

NEW YORK (3): Sid Luckman (Brooklyn); John Mackey (New York City); Art Monk (White Plains).

NORTH CAROLINA (2): Bobby Bell (Shelby); Dwight Stephenson (Murfreesboro).

OHIO (5): Lou Groza (Martins Ferry); Jack Lambert (Mantua); Alan Page (Canton); Roger Staubach (Cincinnati); Paul Warfield (Warren).

OKLAHOMA (2): Steve Largent (Tulsa); Jim Thorpe (Prague).

PENNSYLVANIA (16): Herb Adderley (Philadelphia); Chuck Bednarik (Bethlehem); Fred Biletnikoff (Erie); George Blanda (Youngwood); Mike Ditka (Carnegie); Tony Dorsett (Rochester); Bill George (Waynesburg); Red Grange (Forksville); Jack Ham (Johnstown); Dan Marino (Pittsburgh); Joe Montana (New Eagle); Lenny Moore (Reading); Joe Namath (Beaver Falls); Joe Schmidt (Pittsburgh); Emlen Tunnell (Bryn Mawr); Johnny Unitas

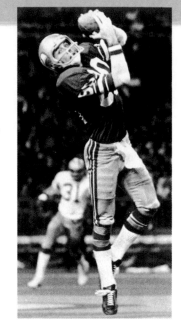
Oklahoman Steve Largent

(Pittsburgh).

SOUTH CAROLINA (1): Art Shell (Charleston).

TENNESSEE (1): Reggie White (Chattanooga).

TEXAS (16): Lance Alworth (Houston); Sammy Baugh (Temple); Raymond Berry (Corpus Christi); Earl Campbell (Tyler); Eric Dickerson (Sealy); Darrell Green (Houston); Joe Greene (Temple); Forrest Gregg (Birthright); Mike Haynes (Denison); Ken Houston (Lufkin); Night Train Lane (Austin); Bobby Layne (Santa Ana); Bob Lilly (Olney); Mike Singletary (Houston); Charley Taylor (Grand Prairie); Gene Upshaw (Robstown).

UTAH (2): Merlin Olsen (Logan); Steve Young (Salt Lake City).

VIRGINIA (5): Roosevelt Brown (Charlottesville); Willie Lanier (Clover); Bruce Smith (Norfolk); Fran Tarkenton (Richmond); Lawrence Taylor (Williamsburg).

WASHINGTON (1): John Elway (Port Angeles).

WEST VIRGINIA (2): Sam Huff (Edna Gas); Gino Marchetti (Smithers).

WISCONSIN (3): Elroy Hirsch (Wausau); Jim Otto (Wausau); Mike Webster (Tomahawk).

OTHER COUNTRIES (3): Ted Hendricks (Guatemala City, Guatemala); Bronko Nagurski (Rainy River, Ontario); Steve Van Buren (La Ceiba, Honduras).

BREAKDOWNS

George Blanda in 1954

(177); Ken Houston (196); Deacon Jones (191); Night Train Lane (157); Steve Largent (200); Bob Lilly (196); Larry Little (183); Ronnie Lott (192); Gino Marchetti (161); Jerry Rice (206); Bruce Smith (201); Emlen Tunnell (167); Randy White (209); Reggie White (216); Steve Young (166).

13—Raymond Berry (154); Roosevelt Brown (163); Buck Buchanan (182); Joe Greene (181); John Hannah (183); Franco Harris (173); Sam Huff (168); Anthony Munoz (185); Joe Namath (140); Walter Payton (190); Joe Schmidt (155); Charley Taylor (165); Lawrence Taylor (184); Paul Warfield (157); Larry Wilson (169).

12—Herb Adderley (164); Bobby Bell (168); Willie Davis (162); Mike Ditka (158); Tony Dorsett (173); Jack Ham (162); Elroy Hirsch (127); Sid Luckman (128); Lenny Moore (143); Mike Singletary (179); Rod Woodson (164).

11—Lance Alworth (136); Lem Barney (140); Eric Dickerson (146); Don Hutson (116); Jack Lambert (146); Willie Lanier (149); Jim Parker (135); O.J. Simpson (135); Roger Staubach (131).

10—Troy Aikman (140); Otto Graham (126); John Mackey (139); Barry Sanders (153); Deion Sanders (133).

9—Jim Brown (118); Dick Butkus (119); Marion Motley (106); Bronko Nagurski (97); Emmitt Smith (140); Kellen Winslow (109).

8—Earl Campbell (115); Jack Christiansen (89); Brett Favre (113); Red Grange (96); Dwight Stephenson (114); Jim Thorpe (52); Steve Van Buren (83).

7—Gale Sayers (68).

TOP 100 ROLL CALL

QUARTERBACKS

Pg.	Player (years)	Born	Died	HOF Election	Pro Bowls	G.	Att.	Comp.	Yds.	TD	Int.	QB Rating	Rush Yards
204	Troy Aikman (1989-present)	11-21-66	——	——	6	140	4,011	2,479	28,346	141	115	82.8	993
30	Sammy Baugh (1937-52)	3-17-14	——	1963	5	165	2,995	1,693	21,886	187	203	72.2	325
210	George Blanda (1949-58; '60-75)	9-17-27	——	1981	4	340	4,007	1,911	26,920	236	277	60.6	344
98	Terry Bradshaw (1970-83)	9-2-48	——	1989	3	168	3,901	2,025	27,989	212	210	70.9	2,257
40	John Elway (1983-present)	6-28-60	——	——	9	234	7,250	4,123	51,475	300	226	79.8	3,407
178	Brett Favre (1991-present)	10-10-69	——	——	5	113	3,757	2,318	26,803	213	118	89.0	1,253
198	Dan Fouts (1973-87)	6-10-51	——	1993	6	181	5,604	3,297	43,040	254	242	80.2	476
22	Otto Graham (1946-55)	12-6-21	——	1965	5	126	2,626	1,464	23,584	174	135	86.6	882
116	Bobby Layne (1948-62)	12-19-26	12-1-86	1967	5	175	3,700	1,814	26,768	196	243	63.4	2,451
88	Sid Luckman (1939-50)	11-21-16	7-5-98	1965	3	128	1,744	904	14,686	137	132	75.0	-239
64	Dan Marino (1983-present)	9-15-61	——	——	9	231	7,989	4,763	58,913	408	235	87.3	93
14	Joe Montana (1979-94)	6-11-56	——	——	8	192	5,391	3,409	40,551	273	139	92.3	1,676
206	Joe Namath (1965-77)	5-31-43	——	1985	5	140	3,762	1,886	27,663	173	220	65.5	140
92	Bart Starr (1956-71)	1-9-34	——	1977	4	196	3,149	1,808	24,718	152	138	80.5	1,308
68	Roger Staubach (1969-79)	2-5-42	——	1985	6	131	2,958	1,685	22,700	153	109	83.4	2,264
130	Fran Tarkenton (1961-78)	2-3-40	——	1986	9	246	6,467	3,686	47,003	342	266	80.4	3,674
18	Johnny Unitas (1956-73)	5-7-33	——	1979	10	211	5,186	2,830	40,239	290	253	78.2	1,777
138	Steve Young (1985-present)	10-11-61	——	——	7	166	4,065	2,622	32,678	229	103	97.6	4,182

RUNNING BACKS

Pg.	Player (years)	Born	Died	HOF Election	Pro Bowls	G.	Att.	Yds.	Avg.	Run TD	Rec.	Yds.	Rec. TD
156	Marcus Allen (1982-97)	3-26-60	——	——	6	221	3,022	12,243	4.1	123	587	5,411	21
10	Jim Brown (1957-65)	2-17-36	——	1971	9	118	2,359	12,312	5.2	106	262	2,499	20
76	Earl Campbell (1978-85)	3-29-55	——	1991	5	115	2,187	9,407	4.3	74	121	806	0
86	Eric Dickerson (1983-93)	9-2-60	——	1999	6	146	2,996	13,259	4.4	90	281	2,137	6
118	Tony Dorsett (1977-88)	4-7-54	——	1994	4	173	2,936	12,739	4.3	77	398	3,554	13
174	Red Grange (1925, '27, '29-34)	6-13-03	1-28-91	1963	——	96	170	569	3.3	21	16	288	10
180	Franco Harris (1972-84)	3-7-50	——	1990	9	173	2,949	12,120	4.1	91	307	2,287	9
154	Lenny Moore (1956-67)	11-25-33	——	1975	7	143	1,068	5,174	4.8	63	363	6,039	48
74	Marion Motley (1946-53, '55)	6-5-20	——	1968	1	106	828	4,720	5.7	31	85	1,107	7
80	Bronko Nagurski (1930-37, '43)	11-3-08	1-7-90	1963	——	97	633	2,778	4.4	25	11	134	——
24	Walter Payton (1975-87)	7-25-54	——	1993	9	190	3,838	16,726	4.4	110	492	4,538	15
32	Barry Sanders (1989-present)	7-16-68	——	——	10	153	3,062	15,269	5.0	99	352	2,921	10
50	Gale Sayers (1965-71)	5-30-43	——	1977	4	68	991	4,956	5.0	39	112	1,307	9
62	O.J. Simpson (1969-79)	7-9-47	——	1985	6	135	2,404	11,236	4.7	61	203	2,142	14
148	Emmitt Smith (1990-present)	5-15-69	——	——	7	140	2,914	12,566	4.3	125	415	2,609	9
190	Jim Thorpe (1920-26, 1928)	5-28-1887	3-28-53	1963	——	52	——	——	——	——	——	——	——
168	Steve Van Buren (1944-51)	12-28-20	——	1965	——	83	1,320	5,860	4.4	69	45	523	3

WIDE RECEIVERS

Pg.	Player (years)	Born	Died	HOF Election	Pro Bowls	G.	Rec.	Yds.	Avg.	TD	Rush Att.	Yds.	Run TD
72	Lance Alworth (1962-72)	8-3-40	——	1978	7	136	542	10,266	18.9	85	24	129	2
90	Raymond Berry (1955-67)	2-27-33	——	1973	5	154	631	9,275	14.7	68	0	0	0
202	Fred Biletnikoff (1965-78)	2-23-43	——	1988	6	190	589	8,974	15.2	76	0	0	0
192	Elroy Hirsch (1946-57)	6-17-23	——	1968	3	127	387	7,029	18.2	60	207	687	4
20	Don Hutson (1935-45)	1-31-13	6-26-97	1963	4	116	488	7,991	16.4	99	62	284	3
214	Charlie Joiner (1969-86)	10-14-47	——	1996	3	239	750	12,146	16.2	65	8	22	0
102	Steve Largent (1976-89)	9-28-54	——	1995	7	200	819	13,089	16.0	100	17	83	1
196	Art Monk (1980-95)	12-5-57	——	——	3	224	940	12,721	13.5	68	63	332	0
12	Jerry Rice (1985-present)	10-13-62	——	——	12	206	1,139	17,612	15.5	164	81	614	10
184	Charley Taylor (1964-77)	9-28-41	——	1984	8	165	649	9,110	14.0	79	442	1,488	11
132	Paul Warfield (1964-77)	11-28-42	——	1983	8	157	427	8,565	20.1	85	22	204	0

TIGHT ENDS

Pg.	Player (years)	Born	Died	HOF Election	Pro Bowls	G.	Rec.	Yds.	Avg.	TD	Att.	Yds.	TD
194	Mike Ditka (1961-72)	10-18-39	——	1988	5	158	427	5,812	13.6	43	2	2	0
106	John Mackey (1963-72)	9-24-41	——	1992	5	139	331	5,236	15.8	38	19	127	0
158	Kellen Winslow (1979-87)	11-5-57	——	1995	5	109	541	6,741	12.5	45	0	0	0

OFFENSIVE LINEMEN

Pg.	Player (years)	Born	Died	HOF Election	Pro Bowls	Key Stats
126	Roosevelt Brown (1953-65)	10-20-32	——	1975	9	163 games; 5 KRs for 32 yds.
66	Forrest Gregg (1956-71)	10-18-33	——	1977	9	193 games; 2 KRs for 21 yds.
212	Lou Groza (1946—59; '61-67)	1-25-24	——	1974	9	268 games; 1,608 points; 264 FGs; 810 extra points.
48	John Hannah (1973-85)	4-4-51	——	1991	9	183 games; 1 KR; 1 fumble TD.
160	Mel Hein (1931-45)	8-22-09	1-31-92	1963	4	170 games; 10 interceptions, 1 TD as LB; 2 receptions.
172	Larry Little (1967-80)	11-2-45	——	1993	5	183 games.
42	Anthony Munoz (1980-92)	8-19-58	——	1998	11	185 games; 7 receptions for 18 yds. and 4 TDs.
170	Jim Otto (1960-74)	1-5-38	——	1980	12	210 games.
56	Jim Parker (1957-67)	4-3-34	——	1973	8	135 games; 1 KR for 15 yds.
122	Art Shell (1968-82)	11-26-46	——	1989	8	207 games; 1 PR.
182	Dwight Stephenson (1980-87)	11-20-57	——	1998	5	114 games.
136	Gene Upshaw (1967-81)	8-15-45	——	1987	7	217 games.
162	Mike Webster (1974-90)	3-18-52	——	1997	9	245 games.

DEFENSIVE BACKS

Pg.	Player (years)	Born	Died	HOF Election	Pro Bowls	G.	Int.	Yds.	TD	Additional Stats
100	Herb Adderley (1961-72)	6-8-39	——	1980	5	164	48	1,046	7	120 KRs, 2 TDs.
208	Lem Barney (1967-77)	9-8-45	——	1992	7	140	56	1,077	7	143 PRs, 50 KRs, 3 TDs; 113 punts.
82	Mel Blount (1970-83)	4-10-48	——	1989	5	200	57	736	2	36 KRs, 1 PR; 2 fumble TDs.
110	Willie Brown (1963-78)	12-2-40	——	1984	9	204	54	472	2	3 PRs, 3 KRs; 1 safety.
186	Jack Christiansen (1951-58)	12-20-28	6-29-86	1970	5	89	46	717	3	85 PRs, 8 TDs; 59 KRs; 2 rush TDs.
176	Darrell Green (1983-present)	2-15-60	——	——	7	234	47	553	6	51 PRs; 2 fumble TDs.
200	Mike Haynes (1976-89)	7-1-53	——	1997	9	177	46	688	2	112 PRs, 2 TDs.
134	Ken Houston (1967-80)	11-12-44	——	1986	12	196	49	898	9	51 PRs, 1 TD; 1 fumble TD.
46	Night Train Lane (1952-65)	4-16-27	——	1974	7	157	68	1,207	5	8 Rec., 1 TD; 1 safety; 1 fumble TD.
54	Ronnie Lott (1981-94)	5-8-59	——	——	10	192	63	730	5	8 KRs.
84	Deion Sanders (1989-present)	8-9-67	——	——	7	133	41	1,094	8	3 Rec. TDs; 8 return TDs; 1 fumble TD.
152	Emlen Tunnell (1948-61)	3-29-22	7-23-75	1967	9	167	79	1,282	4	258 PRs, 5 TDs; 46 KRs, 1 TD.
96	Larry Wilson (1960-72)	3-24-38	——	1978	8	169	52	800	5	1 rush TD; 1 safety; 2 fumble TDs.
188	Rod Woodson (1987-present)	3-10-65	——	——	7	164	47	968	7	2 PR TDs, 2 KR TDs, 1 fumble TD.

LINEBACKERS

Pg.	Player (years)	Born	Died	HOF Election	Pro Bowls	G.	Int.	Yds.	TD	Additional Stats
120	Chuck Bednarik (1949-62)	5-1-25	——	1967	8	169	20	268	1	4 KRs; 12 punts for 483 yds.
144	Bobby Bell (1963-74)	6-17-40	——	1983	9	168	26	479	6	1 KR TD; 2 fumble TDs.
26	Dick Butkus (1965-73)	12-9-42	——	1979	8	119	22	166	0	12 KRs; 1 safety; 1 fumble TD.
108	Bill George (1952-66)	10-27-29	9-30-82	1974	8	173	18	144	0	4 FGs; 14 extra points.
104	Jack Ham (1971-82)	12-23-48	——	1988	8	162	32	218	1	1 fumble TD.
140	Ted Hendricks (1969-83)	11-1-47	——	1990	8	215	26	332	1	4 safeties; 1 fumble TD.
166	Sam Huff (1956-69)	10-4-34	——	1982	5	168	30	381	2	2 fumble TDs.
70	Jack Lambert (1974-84)	7-8-52	——	1990	9	146	28	241	0	
94	Willie Lanier (1967-77)	8-21-45	——	1986	8	149	27	440	2	1 KR; 1 safety.
44	Ray Nitschke (1958-72)	12-29-36	3-8-98	1978	1	190	25	385	2	1 reception for 34 yds.; 6 KRs.
142	Joe Schmidt (1953-65)	1-19-32	——	1973	9	155	24	294	2	1 KR; 1 fumble TD.
124	Mike Singletary (1981-92)	10-9-58	——	1998	10	179	7	44	0	
16	Lawrence Taylor (1981-93)	2-4-59	——	1999	10	184	9	134	2	132.5 sacks.

DEFENSIVE LINEMEN

Pg.	Player (years)	Born	Died	HOF Election	Pro Bowls	Stats
146	Buck Buchanan (1963-75)	9-10-40	7-16-92	1990	8	182 games; 3 interceptions; 1 safety.
150	Willie Davis (1958-69)	7-24-34	——	1981	5	162 games; 2 interceptions; 2 safeties; 1 fumble TD.
36	Joe Greene (1969-81)	9-24-46	——	1987	10	181 games; 1 interception.
34	Deacon Jones (1961-74)	12-9-38	——	1980	8	191 games; 2 KRs; 2 interceptions; 2 safeties.
28	Bob Lilly (1961-74)	7-26-39	——	1980	11	196 games; 1 interception for TD; 3 fumble TDs.
38	Gino Marchetti (1952-66)	1-2-27	——	1972	10	161 games; 1 Rec. TD; 1 interception; 1 safety; 1 fumble TD.
58	Merlin Olsen (1962-76)	9-15-40	——	1982	14	208 games; 1 KR; 1 interception TD.
78	Alan Page (1967-81)	8-7-45	——	1988	9	218 games; 2 interceptions, 1 TD; 3 safeties; 2 fumble TDs.
128	Bruce Smith (1985-present)	6-18-63	——	——	11	201 games; 164 sacks; 2 interceptions; 1 safety; 1 fum. TD.
114	Randy White (1975-88)	1-15-53	——	1994	9	209 games; 1 KR; 1 interception; 52 sacks.
52	Reggie White (1985-98)	12-19-61	——	——	13	216 games; 200.0 sacks; 3 interceptions; 3 fum. TDs; 1 safety.

PHOTO CREDITS

T = top, B = bottom, L = left, R = right, M = middle.

Pages 2-3—NFL Photos; **4**—Vernon J. Biever; **8**—The Sporting News Archives; **10**—Tony Tomsic (L); **10-11**—Tony Tomsic/NFL Photos; **11**—Malcolm W. Emmons (T); **12**—Albert Dickson/The Sporting News; **13**—Mickey Pfleger (T), Albert Dickson/The Sporting News (B); **14**—The Sporting News Archives (T, B); **15**—The Sporting News Archives; **16**—Al Messerschmidt; **17**—The Sporting News Archives (T, B); **18**—Photofile (T), Malcolm W. Emmons (B); **19**—Malcolm W. Emmons; **20**—The Sporting News Archives (T, B); **21**—The Sporting News Archives; **22**—Tony Tomsic/NFL Photos (T), Frank Rippon/NFL Photos (L); **22-23**—Corbis-Bettman; **24**—Al Messerschmidt; **25**—Malcolm W. Emmons (T), Bill Smith/NFL Photos (B); **26**—Malcolm W. Emmons; **27**—Corbis (T), Malcolm W. Emmons (B); **28**—Photofile; **29**—James Flores/NFL Photos (T), The Sporting News Archives (B); **30**—The Sporting News Archives; **30-31**—The Sporting News Archives; **31**—The Sporting News Archives; **32**—The Sporting News Archives (T), Albert Dickson/The Sporting News (B); **33**—Robert Seale/The Sporting News; **34**—Photofile (T), NFL Photos (B); **35**—Malcolm W. Emmons; **36**—Tony Tomsic; **37**—Malcolm W. Emmons (T), Tony Tomsic (B); **38**—The Sporting News Archives (T), NFL Photos (B); **39**—Photofile; **40**—Louis Deluca for The Sporting News; **41**—The Sporting News Archives (T, B); **42**—NFL Photos (T), The Sporting News Archives (B); **43**—Tony Tomsic; **44**—Tony Tomsic/NFL Photos; **44-45**—Vernon J. Biever; **45**—Malcolm W. Emmons; **46**—The Sporting News Archives; **46-47**—Corbis-Bettman; **47**—The Sporting News Archives; **48**—NFL Photos (T), Al Messerschmidt (B); **49**—Tony Tomsic; **50**—Malcolm W. Emmons (T, B); **51**—Malcolm W. Emmons; **52**—The Sporting News Archives (T, B); **53**—Jeff Carlock/Endzone; **54**—The Sporting News Archives; **54-55**—Mickey Pfleger/Endzone; **55**—Mickey Pfleger/Endzone; **56**—The Sporting News Archives; **56-57**—Tony Tomsic; **57**—The Sporting News Archives; **58**—Malcolm W. Emmons; **59**—NFL Photos; **60**—The Sporting News Archives (T, L, R).

Page 62—Robert L. Smith/NFL Photos (T), Malcolm W. Emmons (B); **63**—Malcolm W. Emmons; **64**—Albert Dickson/The Sporting News; **65**—Albert Dickson/The Sporting News (T, B); **66**—Vernon J. Biever; **67**—Vernon J. Biever (T), David Boss/NFL Photos (B); **68**—Malcolm W. Emmons; **69**—Malcolm W. Emmons (T, B); **70**—Malcolm W. Emmons (T, B); **71**—Malcolm W. Emmons; **72**—Tony Tomsic; **73**—Malcolm W. Emmons (T), Tony Tomsic (B); **74**—NFL Photos; **74-75**—Frank Rippon/NFL Photos; **75**—Frank Kuchirchuk/NFL Photos; **76**—Manny Rubio/NFL Photos (T), Al Messerschmidt (B); **77**—Malcolm W. Emmons; **78**—Tony Tomsic; **79**—R.H. Stagg/NFL Photos (T), Malcolm W. Emmons (B); **80**—The Sporting News Archives (T, B); **81**—NFL Photos; **82**—Malcolm W. Emmons/NFL Photos; **83**—R.H. Stagg/NFL Photos (T), Tony Tomsic (B); **84**—Albert Dickson/The Sporting News; **85**—The Sporting News Archives (T, B); **86**—The Sporting News Archives; **87**—The Sporting News Archives (T, B); **88**—NFL Photos; **88-89**—Vic Stein/NFL Photos; **89**—Corbis-Bettman; **90**—The Sporting News Archives (T), Corbis-Bettman (B); **91**—The Sporting News Archives; **92**—Vernon J. Biever/NFL Photos (T), Malcolm W. Emmons (B); **93**—Malcolm W. Emmons; **94**—R.H. Stagg/NFL Photos (T), Tony Tomsic (B); **95**—The Sporting News Archives; **96**—NFL Photos (T), Corbis-Bettman (B); **97**—Tony Tomsic; **98**—Malcolm W. Emmons; **99**—Al Messerschmidt (T), Malcolm W. Emmons (B); **100**—Photofile (T), Vernon J. Biever (B); **101**—John Biever/NFL Photos; **102**—Dave Black/Allsport; **103**—Al Messerschmidt (T, B); **104**—R.H. Stagg/NFL Photos (T), Al Messerschmidt (B); **105**—Malcolm W. Emmons; **106**—NFL Photos; **107**—Tony Tomsic/NFL Photos (T, B); **108**—Frank Rippon/NFL Photos; **109**—The Sporting News Archives (T, B); **110**—NFL Photos (T), The Sporting News Archives (B); **111**—Oakland Raiders; **112**—The Sporting News Archives (TL, TM, TR, B); **113**—The Sporting News Archives (TL, TR, M, B).

Page 114—Malcolm W. Emmons; **115**—Otto Greule/Allsport (T), Malcolm W. Emmons (B); **116**—The Sporting News Archives (T, B); **117**—The Sporting News Archives; **118**—Mickey Pfleger/Endzone; **119**—The Sporting News Archives (T, B); **120**—Vernon J. Biever/NFL Photos; **121**—The Sporting News Archives (T), Photofile (B); **122**—Tony Tomsic; **123**—Tony Tomsic/NFL Photos (T), Tony Tomsic (B); **124**—Malcolm W. Emmons (T, B); **125**—Jonathan Daniel/Allsport; **126**—The Sporting News Archives (T), Dan Rubin/NFL Photos (B); **127**—Photofile; **128**—The Sporting News Archives (T, B); **129**—The Sporting News Archives; **130**—Malcolm W. Emmons; **131**—Malcolm W. Emmons (T, B); **132**—Tony Tomsic; **133**—Malcolm W. Emmons/NFL Photos (T), Malcolm W. Emmons (B); **134**—Nate Fine/NFL Photos (T), Manny Rubio/NFL Photos (B); **135**—Tony Tomsic/NFL Photos; **136**—Tony Tomsic; **137**—R.H Stagg/NFL Photos (T), Tony Tomsic (B); **138**—The Sporting News Archives; **139**—Albert Dickson/The Sporting News (T, B); **140**—Tony Tomsic; **141**—Al Messerschmidt (T), NFL Photos (B); **142**—The Sporting News Archives (T), Photofile (B); **143**—Dave Boss/NFL Photos; **144**—Malcolm W. Emmons; **145**—NFL Photos (T), Malcolm W. Emmons (B); **146**—Malcolm W. Emmons; **147**—NFL Photos (T), The Sporting News Archives (B); **148**—Albert Dickson/The Sporting News; **149**—The Sporting News Archives (T, B); **150**—Tony Tomsic/NFL Photos; **151**—NFL Photos (T, B); **152**—NFL Photos; **152-153**—NFL Photos; **153**—The Sporting News Archives; **154**—NFL Photos; **154-155**—Vernon J. Biever; **155**—Photofile; **156**—Robert Seale/The Sporting News; **156-157**—The Sporting News Archives; **157**—The Sporting News Archives; **158**—Dan Honda/NFL Photos (T), Al Messerschmidt (B); **159**—Andy Hayt/NFL Photos; **160**—The Sporting News Archives (T, B); **161**—The Sporting News Archives; **162**—NFL Photos (T), Malcolm W. Emmons (B); **163**—Al Messerschmidt.

Page 166—Dan Rubin/NFL Photos; **167**—The Sporting News Archives (T), Malcolm W. Emmons (B); **168**—The Sporting News Archives; **168-169**—NFL Photos; **169**—The Sporting News Archives; **170**—Malcolm W. Emmons; **170-171**—Malcolm W. Emmons; **171**—Malcolm W. Emmons; **172**—Tony Tomsic/NFL Photos; **173**—Al Messerschmidt (T, B); **174**—The Sporting News Archives; **175**—NFL Photos (T), The Sporting News Archives (B); **176**—Robert Seale/The Sporting News; **176-177**—The Sporting News Archives; **177**—Robert Seale/The Sporting News; **178**—Albert Dickson/The Sporting News (T, B); **179**—The Sporting News Archives; **180**—George Gojkovich/Allsport (T), Malcolm W. Emmons (B); **181**—Malcolm W. Emmons; **182**—Al Messerschmidt; **182-183**—Al Messerschmidt; **183**—Al Messerschmidt; **184**—Clifton Boutelle/NFL Photos; **185**—NFL Photos (T), Tony Tomsic/NFL Photos (B); **186**—The Sporting News Archives (T), Vernon J. Biever/NFL Photos (B); **187**—George Gellatly/NFL Photos; **188**—John Dunn for The Sporting News; **188-189**—Al Messerschmidt; **189**—John Dunn for The Sporting News; **190**—NFL Photos; **191**—Allsport (T), The Sporting News Archives (B); **192**—The Sporting News Archives; **192-193**—The Sporting News Archives; **193**—The Sporting News Archives; **194**—Darryl Norenberg/NFL Photos (T, B); **195**—Malcolm W. Emmons; **196**—Tony Tomsic; **197**—Al Messerschmidt (T), Damian Strohmeyer/Allsport (B); **198**—Malcolm W. Emmons; **199**—Pete J. Groh/NFL Photos (T), Peter Read Miller/NFL Photos (B); **200**—Photofile; **201**—NFL Photos (T), The Sporting News Archives (B); **202**—NFL Photos (T), Al Messerschmidt (B); **203**—Tony Tomsic; **204**—The Sporting News Archives (T, B); **205**—Albert Dickson/The Sporting News; **206**—Malcolm W. Emmons (T, B); **207**—Malcolm W. Emmons; **208**—NFL Photos (T), Tony Tomsic/NFL Photos (B); **209**—Manny Rubio/NFL Photos; **210**—Photofile; **210-211**—Russ Reed/NFL Photos; **211**—R.H. Stagg/NFL Photos; **212**—NFL Photos; **212-213**—Tony Tomsic; **213**—Tony Tomsic; **214**—Al Messerschmidt (T, B); **215**—Tony Tomsic; **216**—The Sporting News Archives; **217**—The Sporting News Archives; **219**—The Sporting News Archives (T, B); **222-223**—TSN Archives.